Working together:
Carer participation in England, Wales and Northern Ireland

Alan Roulstone, Val Hudson, Jeremy Kearney and Ailsa Martin, with Jon Warren

First published in Great Britain in June 2006
by the Social Care Institute for Excellence

ISBN-10 1-904812-35-X
ISBN-13 1-904812-35-7

Written by Alan Roulstone, Val Hudson, Jeremy Kearney and Ailsa Martin,
with Jon Warren

Produced by The Policy Press
Fourth Floor, Beacon House
Queen's Road
Bristol BS8 1QU
tel 0117 331 4054
fax 0117 331 4093
tpp-info@bristol.ac.uk
www.policypress.org.uk

This report is available in print and online
www.scie.org.uk

Social Care Institute for Excellence
Goldings House
2 Hay's Lane
London SE1 2HB
tel 020 7089 6840
fax 020 7089 6841
textphone 020 7089 6893
www.scie.org.uk

Front cover photograph kindly supplied by www.JohnBirdsall.co.uk

Acronyms

ADSS	Association of Directors of Social Services
BME	black and minority ethnic
CMHN	community mental health nurse
CADI	Carers' Assessment of Difficulty Index
CASI	Carers' Assessment of Satisfaction Index
CPA	care programme approach
CPN	community psychiatric nurse
CPRG	carer participation research group
CSDW	carer support and development worker
CSW	carer support worker
DH	Department of Health
ELSC	Electronic Library in Social Care
EMI	elderly/mentally infirm
ESF	European Social Fund
GP	general practitioner
HAZ	Health Action Zone
ICT	information and communications technology
JCT	joint commissioning trust
LA	local authority
LDPB	learning disability partnership board
LGB or LGBT	lesbian, gay and bisexual (and transgender)
LIT	local implementation team
MARG	modernisation and reform group
MRC	Medical Research Council
MS	multiple sclerosis
NHS	National Health Service
NSF	national service framework
OT	occupational therapist
PALS	Patient Advisory Liaison Service
PB	partnership board
PCT	primary care trust
SCIE	Social Care Institute for Excellence
SIGLE	System for Information on Grey Literature in Europe
SNAQ	Southampton Needs Assessment Questionnaire
SOSIG	Social Science Information Gateway
SRB	Single Regeneration Budget
SSD	social services department
SSI	Social Services Inspectorate
TPCT	teaching primary care trust
WAG	Welsh Assembly Government

Acknowledgements

The authors would like to acknowledge the help and support given to this Position Paper. First, to Ailsa Martin (Princess Royal Trust for Carers) and the staff and carers at Sunderland Carers' Centre for their unstinting support in the framing, delivery and monitoring of the position paper. Specific thanks go to Margaret Cutter for her excellent administrative and liaison skills. The insights of all these individuals have been invaluable in providing the required nuances with which to understand the carer experience.

A key part of the paper's methodology was the creation of a 'carers' participation reference group' that provided significant carer insights with which to revise and tighten the research focus. Thanks go to Jenny Cook, Charlie Telling, James King, Dorothy Dobinson, Anne Harvey, Alan Lindsley and Gill Charman.

Thanks are also extended to members of the review group who provided national insights around policy, practice and carer experiences across England, Wales and Northern Ireland. Many thanks are given to: Linda Cooper of Carers First and Department of Health adviser in the Learning Disability Support Team; Margaret Fletcher of the Princess Royal Trust; Tom Coard, Belfast Carers Centre; Stephen Yorke, Carers Wales; and Alicia Christian of the Princess Royal Trust for Carers Centre in Sandwell.

Additional thanks to Pamela Jupp, Gill Davison and Diane Scott and to CLASP: The Carers Centre in Leicester and Suffolk County Council, for their valuable input into the project.

Summary of key findings

Literature review

- There is a diversity of carer participation taking place.
- Carer participation is construed as ranging from consultation to direct involvement in shaping the outcome of carer services.
- There is as yet no consensus on the theoretical understanding or shared meaning of what 'carer participation' means.
- Most studies on carer participation focus on consultation-type activities; far fewer concentrate on carers making a difference to service design, delivery and review.
- Most research and writing is based on small-scale qualitative studies. These are valuable but tell us little about the broader, quantitative picture of carer participation.
- Strategic-level involvement is growing in significance. However, the evidence of this benefiting individual carers is limited.
- The collective representation of carers' voices is less often in evidence than the voices of what might be called 'expert carers'. Paradoxically, the closer these carers get to strategic decision making, the greater the risk of an inadvertent distancing from street-level experiences of ordinary carers.
- Studies of carer assessments, while suggesting greater awareness and use of such assessments, indicate that their use is patchy and that outcomes where assessments take place are often limited or sometimes not forthcoming.
- Respite care is central to carers developing greater autonomy and having a break from the strain of caring. However, the literature fairly unanimously indicates a shortfall of provision against carer expectations.
- Few studies focus on statutory follow-up activities after participation has taken place. This might suggest that the maturation process of carer participation is far from complete.
- There are some examples in the literature that point to creative joint commissioning and provision of carer participation support. These chiefly involve social services department (SSD), primary care trust (PCT) and learning disability partnership board (LDPB) joint working.
- Some of the most innovative activity is being funded and provided by SSDs, PCTs and health trusts – for example, in the mental health and learning disability areas.
- Perhaps the most developed forms of carer participation include involvement of carers in key recruitment roles for posts related to carer participation and major programme review and change.
- The literature that includes black and minority ethnic (BME) carers is growing, but there are few studies of BME carers' involvement *per se*. The evidence available suggests that BME carers are more likely to be involved in consultation than in fully fledged participation activity.
- Cultural assumptions that BME communities look after their own are pervasive in BME carer literature.
- There was very limited literature on the participation and recognition of gay and lesbian carers.
- There is limited crossover between voluntary sector and academic research. Very few academic studies cite the major quantitative studies available in the voluntary sector.

Practice Survey

- There are examples of creative and supportive carer participation activities in both statutory and voluntary contexts.
- As with the literature review findings, the coverage of consultation activity is significant, covering most statutory organisations.
- Carer participation in service planning and review seems to be happening at a strategic level and, where undertaken, is successful in including the voices and aspirations of some carers.
- Carers' organisations are playing a key role in activating and substantiating carer participation legislation and guidance. These activities are funded by the Carers Grant and additional finance is received from major national voluntary sector providers and, occasionally, European Social Fund (ESF) or Single Regeneration Budget (SRB) funding.
- The most mature carer participation schemes involve carers at both strategic and street level and include feedback mechanisms that ensure that carer input makes a difference to service delivery.
- Some statutory organisations are involving carers in key appointments and in contracting and assessment protocol decisions.
- Some statutory organisations express the view that where targets have been set – for example, in *Valuing people* and the National Service Framework (NSF) for mental health – there is more carer participation. However, according to the survey findings, there is a risk that carer issues outside key statutory targets may not be addressed.
- More could be done to identify and include the participation of historically 'hidden' or marginalised carers. Not surprisingly, some of the most innovative work is being undertaken in areas of significant ethnic and cultural diversity.
- Carers feel that firmer guidance and adherence measures are needed to ensure that carer assessments are completed and acted on. More could be done to make carers aware of their rights to an assessment.
- In the authorities studied, emergency planning for carer absence or loss is limited. Most efforts currently revolve around temporary loss of carer due to illness. Wider guidance and awareness is felt to be needed, especially in situations where carers pre-decease the person cared for.
- Funding and professional/organisational cultures are seen as militating against consistent partnership working. Some organisations, especially health trusts, are felt not to perceive such participation work as 'core business'.
- Some of the most creative inputs to carer-centred work is being undertaken by PCTs, with some trusts supporting substantial staffing input. Paradoxically, PCTs and health trusts are also more likely to state that carers are not seen as 'core business' and are often funded with 'soft money' (non-recurrent funding).
- Some in the statutory sector feel that more guidance networks would be useful in cementing best practice ideas into service standards and delivery.
- Some local authorities (LAs) are using 'modernisation and reform groups' (MARGs) to embed their carer participation work in a successful way. This ensures cross-departmental working in a more seamless way.
- The area in which expectation and delivery are most mismatched is in the area of carer assessment.

1 Introduction

This Position Paper is the result of work undertaken by the University of Sunderland and the Sunderland Carers' Centre (part of the Princess Royal Trust for Carers). It is premised on the belief that carers are experts in their own lives, and that their participation in service planning and delivery should lead to improvement in those services.

The Position Paper has been carer-led from the outset. Carers have had a key role in focusing on the methods adopted, formulating research instruments, reviewing the progress of the work, undertaking matched interviews with carers and appraising draft copies of the document. Carers in both London and Belfast have been involved in showcasing the work as it developed. Partnership principles and a participatory research paradigm have been adopted as the basis of the study and a wider Position Paper.

In addition, the researchers wanted to establish the principles of carer participation through the research process. To conduct the research for this paper, it was agreed to establish three groups:

- **The research team** This team has worked together for some time. One member is the coordinator of the Sunderland Carers' Centre. She has a lot of experience in working with many different groups of carers, both locally and nationally. The other three members are from the University of Sunderland. Two of them have considerable research experience, including work with carers and service users: the lead researcher is an expert in disability and user involvement and has been a service user for the past 20 years. The other has many years of experience in a social services department (SSD), has worked with carers and is a carer herself.
- **Carer participation reference group (CPRG)** This group of carers for adults was brought together by the research team and Sunderland Carers' Centre. It was made up of a wide range of people, including black and minority ethnic carers (BME), gay/lesbian carers and others who themselves were disabled. The Sunderland Carers' Centre defines a carer as 'a person who looks after someone who, due to illness, disability or frailty, is unable to manage alone. This may be a relative, neighbour or friend'. This group wished to make sure that the research team looked at the things that are important to carers, and that carers would be able to understand what the research is saying.
- **Review steering group** This group included people from all over the country, to make sure that the research took account of what is happening nationally. It included 10 carers and carer stakeholders from diverse backgrounds (including BME and LGBT [lesbian, gay, bisexual and transgender carers]) and the four members of the research team. The main purpose of this group was to ensure that the research team was carrying out the research according to the agreed protocol and that the work met the timetable.

Full details of carer involvement can be found in Appendix A.

1.1 The Position Paper

The Position Paper is made up of two complementary elements: a literature review and a practice survey. Both of these consist of a range of elements detailed below.

1.1.1 The literature review

There are two key elements to the literature review. The first is a *systematic review of published material* on carer participation. Most of the publications reviewed are studies or action research projects of carer participation that meet minimum academic standards of robust and transparent research methods. Where they are theoretical or conceptual in character, they demonstrate an engagement with the broader canon of thinking. Most articles will have been peer or editorially reviewed. The dates of study and the research methods are available (*see* Section 3).

The exact level of independence from the organisation, initiative or project being studied does, of course, vary. Some studies are 'in-house' or with known social care and/or clinical colleagues. Anonymous peer review helps ensure the robustness and objectivity of the studies presented. The systematic review has tight inclusion, time and thematic parameters. All constituent studies or conceptual materials for the systematic review are presented in the annotated bibliography (Appendix B).

The second element of the literature review consists of *illustrative examples of carer participation taken from 'grey' (unpublished) literature*. These help provide an idea of the scope and range of good practice projects that attempt to enhance carer participation activity. The 'illustrative examples' are gleaned from unpublished reports, public information materials, organisational plans, strategies and reviews and from organisational website content. The examples present carer participation projects and initiatives from both the statutory and the voluntary sectors, some of which involve close working across the sectors. The materials are uncorroborated and not peer reviewed for content, currency or accuracy. By including them, we aim to provide an illustrative picture of the range and type of carer participation work. In this section, organisations are named as the information presented is already in the public domain with organisational attribution made known (*see* Section 4). Website addresses are provided for each of these examples.

1.1.1.1 Terminology and language use

The term 'carer participation' is used inclusively to embrace consultation, information sharing, carer involvement in service planning and review and, ultimately, direct carer impact on the nature, shape and enhancement of services for carers. It is recognised that much best practice in carer participation is likely to link into similar practice with service users. For the purposes of the literature review, however, the principal focus was on the experiences, perceptions, roles and voices of carers in shaping their experiences of care services, support and planning. The terms 'carer involvement' and 'carer inclusion' as close synonyms are also used to ensure that inadvertent omission from the literature review is minimised.

1.1.1.2 Involving carers: research values and philosophy

This Position Paper has aimed in its entirety to involve carers in all key aspects of the research that underpins it. Following Zarb (1) and Shaw in Kemshall and Littlechild (2), the paper and its constituent research are based on a *participatory* research paradigm that sees non-professional research participants and advisers as central to the relations of research production. Research here aims to empower carers but sees any simple relationship between paid researchers and carers as problematic. Here, empowerment is not perceived as a process of giving power directly, but as providing the circumstances in which carers (and also disabled people and service users) can empower themselves (3). The research team and carers felt that the findings of the paper would more likely open up the array and depth of carers' issues by the fullest involvement of carers throughout. Empowerment in research, as propounded in the work of Jack (4) and Oliver (5), can only take place where professional researchers relinquish some degree of control over the social relations of research production. This is echoed in very recent research by Hanley and the Toronto Group (6).

The term and notion 'emancipatory research' was not felt appropriate for this paper as it was believed that this term would make greater claims for the impact of the paper than were strictly achievable. It was also felt that emancipation is a process and not a fixed state, one that is open to many future influences. This is not to argue that the model or paradigm is unworkable. It is just that emancipation is only likely to occur where an action research framework allows significant personal and social impact. It is hoped, however, that this paper, with the involvement of carers in its creation, will change carers' lives, however hard it will be to quantify that impact.

Although the Social Care Institute for Excellence (SCIE) provided the framework and focus for the paper, carers have been involved from the outset, and have:

- aided the focusing of the paper and its remit, methods and definition of adult carers
- designed the key research tools, including questionnaires and interview schedules
- advised on which areas of community and clinical activity required appraisal in terms of carer participation
- taken an active and executive role in reviewing all aspects of the paper through a carer participation review group (local group of carers) and a national review group made up of carers and key stakeholders in social care
- taken an active part in advising on the interviewing of carers and carers centre staff
- advised on carer diversity and inclusivity to ensure that BME, LGBT, older and lifetime carers are accounted for in the paper and also that carers of often forgotten user groups are included – for example, those with drug and/or alcohol problems
- appraised the quantitative and qualitative findings of the paper
- commented on and asked for amendments to the draft paper
- commented on SCIE feedback and established a dialogue between carers, the research team and SCIE
- educated and advised the research team as to the time required to fully involve carers.

1.1.2 The practice survey

The second element of the Position Paper is a comprehensive practice survey. This has taken the form of a survey of statutory and voluntary practices around carer participation. SSDs, primary care trusts (PCTs) and health trusts, learning disability partnership boards (LDPBs), joint health and social care boards/trusts, carers' centres and carers were surveyed in England, Wales and Northern Ireland using a detailed semi-structured questionnaire format. Selective interviews were undertaken to reflect geographical, practice and population diversity (for example, ethnicity, rural versus urban).

In addition to statutory stakeholders, questionnaires were sent to carers' centres, voluntary sector carer (or care-inclusive) organisations – for example, Carers UK, the Princess Royal Trust, Rethink, the Alzheimer's Society, Age Concern and the Afiya Trust. Selective interviews were held with the staff of an illustrative number of carers' organisations and then with carers themselves. Organisational and personal carer details are kept anonymous in this section of the Position Paper as the data was gathered under conditions of confidentiality (*see* Section 5).

1.2 Background and context to the Position Paper

There is now an established literature on the economic and social value provided by informal and unpaid carers (7-13). The strong association between informal caring and social exclusion have also been acknowledged in academic and policy circles (14-21). There is evidence of the particular social and economic disadvantage of BME carers, given both pre-existing economic disadvantage (22-24) and lack of immediate family networks (25, 26). The intersection of disability and ethnicity also present problems for traditional service categories that fail to respond to the multifaceted nature of oppression and rights (27-32). Evidence suggests that the Carers Grant, an important policy tool for promoting independence (8), has often not been earmarked for 'hidden carer' communities who may benefit most from the short breaks that the grant is designed to support (33). Policy and practice assumptions that BME communities 'look after their own' may in part explain this oversight (34, 35).

Evidence also points to the health implications of informal caring (36-41). The group perhaps least well served by care services and most likely to be hidden from view are lesbian and gay carers (42-44), given the still prevalent nature of homophobia and professional perceptions of the rights of same-sex partners.

Recent demographic analyses point to the likely growth in spousal caring and the increased incidence in later-life family caring situations (45-50). Demographic changes offer more specific policy challenges in terms of the greater number of service users with dementia (51-53) and degenerative neurological conditions and the number of people with learning difficulties living into older age (54).

Feminist debates on gender and caring have pointed to concerns that women have historically borne a disproportionate weight of caring responsibilities (5-58). While acknowledging the continued gender asymmetry in caring, more recent work points to the significant diversity of carers and carer responsibilities in terms of age, gender, ethnicity, sexual orientation, cultural affiliations, health, social capital and disability (15, 25, 59-61). There is now quite clear evidence that many (diverse) carers face significant barriers accessing the support to which they are entitled (62-69). Any simple formula based on single-stranded theories of 'carer burden' needs to be treated with caution, given carer diversity and the dynamic nature of the caring relationship (18). Indeed, new dimensions of carer exclusion are beginning to be highlighted – for example, Manthorpe's research, 'Caring at a distance' (70), highlights the practice issues of accounting for carers who travel long distances to care for relatives.

Another potentially unplanned impact on informal carers is the increased use of 'day case' surgery, and the likely extra personal and sometimes unmet clinical care needs that may fall to informal carers (71). Evidence to date on the interface between hospital discharge and carer needs is not promising (37, 72). Emergency planning and replacement care if a carer is ill or dies remains a major concern for carer organisations, with one recent study noting that only 20 of the 150 English local authorities (LAs) have a carers' emergency scheme in place (73).

The above highlights then the imperative to address issues of carers' involvement in the services that shape their lives. Put simply, carer participation may make the difference between tolerable and unsustainable caring situations.

Despite the above challenges, there is much promise in developments during the past 15 years in our thinking about the needs and rights of carers. New ways of regarding the rights of carers emerged from carer organisations and social care writers (74, 75). Although the position and rights of users and carers have not always been viewed as complementary, the language and logic of carer involvement was directly informed by user involvement ideas, the user movement and the burgeoning UK disabled people's movement (2, 18, 76-82). Recent commentary suggests that, with sufficient voice and involvement, both carers and service users can work together in changing services in a way that supports both (18).

In England, the advent of the Carers (Recognition and Services) Act 1995 (83), the carers' national strategy *Caring for carers* (1999) (84), the Carers and Disabled Children Act 2000 (85), the Community Care (Delayed Discharges, etc) Act 2003 (86) and, most recently, the Carers (Equal Opportunities) Act 2004 (87) all give reference to participation in the planning, assessment and review of support for carers. Similarly, the Community Care (Direct Payments) Act 1996 (88) aims to include carers by allowing them to purchase services they are assessed as needing, to support them in their caring role. However, the only national service framework (NSF) to specifically mention carers is the 1999 NSF for mental health (89). *Valuing people* (90), the key modernisation document for learning difficulties, has a chapter that refers to carers and the importance of their role in supporting people with learning difficulties.

Early studies of the efficacy of the carers' national strategy point to the increased incidence of consultation. However, many of the carers researched had not been involved in any consultation, while carers having a significant role in planning and reviewing services remained a rare phenomenon three years after the introduction of the strategy (91, 92). More recent research paints a similar picture of professionals failing to respond to carers' longer-term concerns about their ability to care in the future (93).

Despite these continued limitations, involvement of carers in service design, review and delivery are now key statutory expectations with substantive rights attached. For example, the Carers (Recognition and Services) Act 1995 gives carers access to an assessment in their own right, while the Carers and Disabled Children Act 2000 further extends the inclusion and participation of carers by affording substantive rights to packages of assessed support even where service users refuse an assessment. The practice guidance that accompanies the Act (Department of Health, 2001b, paraphrased below) (95) makes clear in its guiding principles the need to shift practice towards:

- improvements in the identification of carers
- improvements in the process of assessing the impact of the carer's role
- effective use of the Framework for the Assessment of Children and Families in Need
- greater recognition of carers and increased listening to them about the outcomes they would like following assessment
- innovation in meeting assessed needs
- pragmatic assessments, avoiding bureaucracy and focusing on what the carer sees as the required outcome
- holistic, integrated, family-based assessment that sees carers and cared-for people as partners in the caring relationship.

The wider guidance makes clear the imperative need for:

- multi agency information sharing
- maximum LA coordination in joining up care and carer provision with wider legislation, guidance and services
- the identification by commissioners of the fullest range of available local services
- appropriate staff training
- carer surveys
- growing awareness of the employment commitments and aspirations of some carers.

For the purpose of this paper, what is less clear in the guidance to the 2000 Act are the key performance indicators to use in establishing a successful response to carer participation. However, further direction is provided in the Department of Health's *Beacon status scheme 2005, round 6: Supporting carers* (96) literature that makes clear how excellent practice is evaluated in a LA context. Drawing on the work of Banks and Cheeseman (97), consultation and involvement are cited as important in providing carers a voice in commissioning, inspection and monitoring processes. A number of examples of best practice are provided. While these awards attest to the improvements being made in some localities, and wider evidence suggests that involvement and partnership with carers is increasing, the rate of change and growth of awareness among statutory professionals is disappointing (98).

The current picture from the published literature suggests that carer participation and involvement is clearly on the agenda, but the extent to which it is functioning and monitored and impacts outcomes and the lives of carers is still open to question. One clear policy paradox is that tight budgetary allocations are to the fore in the practice of social care professionals at the same time as they are being encouraged to engage carers more fully (2, 99-101). An attendant question is the extent to which carers' views – for example, on carer assessment – are being formulated into service metrics that equate to firm service outcomes (102).

The Carers (Equal Opportunities) Act 2004 aims to ensure that carers are able to take up social and economic opportunities – for instance, paid employment, training and lifelong learning – that non-carers may take for granted. While there is limited hard evidence on the educational and training costs of informal caring, there is an established literature on the employment challenges of combining informal care with paid employment (103-110).

The Act will require that carers are made aware of their statutory right to an assessment, and that partnership working is required between health services and local government in meeting the needs of carers. While the Act emanated from a private member's Bill, the government's commitment to supporting carers in paid employment stems from the carers' national strategy *Caring for carers*, launched in 1999 (84), which showed how carers could prosper in both roles with sufficient support. Specific embodiment of the commitment to aiding working carers to maintain both roles is evident in the National Health Service (NHS) workforce strategy for informal carers. Two key initiatives supported this: first, the Employment Relations Act 1999 (111), which extended the rights of employees to take time off in an emergency to discharge caring responsibilities; and second, the 'Work–Life Balance' initiative that was introduced in March 2000. This, too, has clear potential in assisting carers to maintain a work–life balance.

In Northern Ireland, the hub of carer participation commitment is contained within the Department of Health, Social Services and Public Safety's Carers and Direct Payments Act (Northern Ireland) 2002 (112), and by the major review of carers' support *Valuing carers* (113). More recently the foundations of carer support have been strengthened by the consultation in Northern Ireland on *Standards to improve quality in health and social care* (114). Northern Ireland is not directly comparable to England and Wales as it:

- has long-established joint health and social care boards and trusts
- does not have a Carers Grant allocation
- is not duty bound by the Carers (Equal Opportunities) Act 2004.

However, the above legislation and public commitment to involving and supporting carers has recently been reaffirmed by the Northern Ireland Social Services Inspectorate's (SSIs) *Final draft standards for inspection of social care support services for carers of older people* (115). Following from and adopting the earlier *Valuing carers* principles, the inspection standards highlight that:

- carers are real and equal partners
- carers need flexible and responsive support
- carers have a right to a life outside caring
- caring should be freely chosen
- the government should invest in caring.

Research evidence on carer participation and involvement in Northern Ireland is, however, very sparse. An exception is research by Halliday and Dixon, which explored carer and user perceptions of consultation in the construction of care packages (116).

In Wales, the *Caring about carers* strategy (117), the development of the *Carer's strategy implementation plan* in July 2000 (118), the *Adult mental health strategy* (119) and Standard 2 of the NSF for working-age adults and work with BME carers (120) all attest to the commitment to involving carers in service planning, delivery and review. The Welsh Assembly Government (WAG) Adult Mental Health Services policy implementation guide (121) provides a conceptual and policy framework with which to apply empowerment principles to working with carers in partnership. Much statutory and voluntary sector partnership working is under way ahead of the mainstreaming of the Carers Grant into the general Revenue Support Grant in 2006. A number of inferences can be drawn from the timing of this growth in carer participation activity.

The above points to a range of statutory factors that, in principle, make participation more likely. What is less clear are levels of effectiveness and depths of commitment that attach to partnership working and participation in practice and at street level. 'Third way' policy and the communitarian emphasis on 'rights and responsibilities' at the heart of New Labour policy reforms have helped embed citizen involvement in a wide range of policy and practice areas. Additionally, emphasis on joined-up government has led to significant policy stress on seamless working across departmental and service boundaries (16, 122-124), which also needs to be reflected in any meaningful planning for participation. This emphasis on joined-up government is embodied in the enhanced role of the Cabinet Office and, specifically, the Prime Minister's Strategy Unit in making cross-departmental policy connections. The voices of local communities are centre stage in many of the aspirations of the New Labour government, as, for example, in the White Paper *Modern local government – In touch with the people* (107).

Although carers can be seen as attracting significant policy and academic attention (125-128), at present we know too little about the extent, quality and efficacy of user or carer participation in the planning, review and enhancement of social care services. This mirrors findings on user involvement (129). We also need to know much more about good or best practice: what it is taken to mean, and how it is achieved and sustained. Do different street-level interpretations of 'best practice' exist or are there significant overlaps in our understanding? If valuable lessons about participation are to be learned, we need to be able to identify the origins, drivers and facilitators of successful partnership. Clearly there is a need to understand the extent to which wider policy initiatives – for example, 'Best value' – are commensurate with carer participation where the latter may import different values that focus primarily on service quality rather than cost (130). There is an urgent need to reflect the participation needs and experiences of carers and to place this within a relational context that empowers both carer and service user.

The SCIE Position Paper on user participation (129) clearly identified the role of power in influencing the impact of service users on care planning and review (131-133). Both successful and more limited participation initiatives need to be understood in terms of power relations. Are successful participation approaches due to the significant relinquishing of power by social services and voluntary sector professionals? How important have power dynamics been in terms of aiding or limiting successful participation? We know that empowerment is rarely if ever a positive-sum game in power terms (4, 126, 134-136) and that user and carer empowerment in substantive terms has to involve the transfer of power in ideas, resources and decision making (137-141). Some commentators have asserted that power sharing need not conflict with good carer/user and practitioner relations (138). Indeed, the history of the interface between the most radical challenges to existing professional power has itself been marked by the apparent cooperation between these radical organisations and the statutory and voluntary sectors (79, 142, 143). The redistribution of power is also an issue in academic and clinical research, which is seen by some writers as based on research relationships that have reflected wider social inequalities and professional power (2). Specific criticisms attach to research on disabled people and people with learning difficulties as it has often been based on a 'personal tragedy' or medical model of disability (5, 144).

The redistribution of power is one key element of empowerment of carers (102), while in some areas, such as dementia care, early diagnosis is seen as a prerequisite of power sharing as often no service interventions occur pre-diagnosis (145). Ryan and Bamber completed research evaluating the role of expenses payments in encouraging user and carer involvement. Part of that study design was to identify how payments could be used strategically to further future involvement – for example, by paying for both carer time and attendance expenses. In power terms, they found that most expenses policies were initiated by managers and users/carers; however, the writing of the policies was more likely to be completed by managers and practitioners (146). This may help carers 'set agendas' and ignore benefit traps that some face in balancing benefits and expenses.

In addition to understanding participation and identifying a range of practice in carer involvement and the power relations of participation, the literature review and practice survey aim to draw out the complex interplay between carer diversity, organisational support and susceptibility to 'hidden carer' status. Here, the experience of being a black, gay/lesbian, older or disabled carer needs to be fully reflected in both the literature review and the practice survey. It is crucially important that carers who may face multiple types of oppression in their wider lives are fully accounted for in their views of carer participation.

The assumption that BME families may take the weight of care needs within an extended family (147), the assumption that the needs of older or disabled carers and service users are fully met with the advent of the Carers (Recognition and Services) Act 1995 and the assumption that the carers of disabled children have had their needs met with the accession of the Carers and Disabled Children Act 2000 all need to be questioned. The insights that already exist around black (African or Caribbean) carers (148, 149), disabled and older carers (148-150) and gay/lesbian carers (43) all need to be factored into an evaluation of carer participation. Only by including these cross-cutting insights can the full diversity of power dynamics be understood in the participation equation.

2 Carer participation studies: the scope of the literature review

The primary search strategy for the formal literature review has been to conduct a systematic literature review of the following computerised databases: Electronic Library in Social Care (ELSC), ASSIA,C2 SPECTR (Campbell Collaboration), Cochrane Library, Cinahl, IBSS, ISI Web of Knowledge, Journals Online (TandF), PsycINFO, PubMed, CSA Illumina/Sociological Abstracts, Social Work Abstracts, Social Services Abstracts and Zetoc. These databases were chosen to reflect the widest range of literature available and because they were held in electronic form by the University of Sunderland library (*see* Appendix C for details of databases searched). The Social Science Information Gateway (SOSIG) was used to gain access to key carer documents, legislation and guidance. The non-peer-reviewed practice journal *Community Care* was searched using the full key search terms. The HMIC database and Wilson Social Science Abstracts were not searched as they were not available through subscription to the University of Sunderland or were in print format only. The research team deployed OVID SIGLE to explore 'grey' (that is, unpublished) literature. Hand searches of journals was also undertaken (*see* Appendix D). Additionally, major caring organisation websites were trawled for grey literature; a complete list of organisations contacted is given in Appendix E.

The principal selection criterion was the relevance of the material to addressing the central research question: 'What are the factors that encourage the highest possible quality of participation of carers in the delivery of social care?'. In the research, 'social care' has been defined broadly to mean all those areas of health and social care where services impinge on carers and the people they care for. As a result of feedback from the CPRG in the early part of the research, the focus of the research was broadened to include acute medical services as well as PCTs. These aspects are also part of the overall research in that interviews took place with individuals in SSDs, PCTs, health authorities, partnership boards (PBs) and voluntary organisations.

Therefore, the initial scoping exercise aimed to cover a broad range of material in order to 'map' the literature that currently exists in the relevant areas and to report on the most relevant studies to address the different aspects of the research question. These included: levels of carer participation in service developments, carers' views on participation in services, barriers to participation and examples of current or past projects that represent best practice in carer participation.

2.1 Identifying relevant material: outline details

A number of key terms were used for the database searches using a Boolean search methodology adopting AND and WITH combinations of:

- carer(s)
- carer participation
- carer inclusion
- carer involvement
- carer planning

- carer review
- carer partnerships
- carer agreements
- carer assessment
- caregiver/s.

And where databases facilitated this, the following search terms were used:

- carer AND/WITH black and minority ethnic
- carer AND/WITH gay
- carer AND/WITH lesbian
- carer AND/WITH lesbian, gay, bisexual.

A full delineation of the article summary sheet and search methods used can be found in Appendices F and G.

2.1.1 Inclusion criteria

- The reference specifically related to research, an initiative or a project that included some involvement of carers.
- If a theoretical piece, it must have included some discussion or analysis of issues of carer involvement or participation.
- The reference was dated between 1993 and April 2005.
- The reference related to work carried out in England, Wales and/or Northern Ireland. Work based in Scotland was only used where research would translate into the UK more widely or had been piloted in England.
- The reference was in English or translated from Welsh.

The database search identified a total of 29,913 references, 335 of which were marked and an abstract obtained. The large number of hits is explicable in that a significant number of articles identified as carer participation had titles that contained the phrase 'user and carer'. In many cases, these articles and studies were largely about users with carers treated inadvertently as 'add-ons'. Other articles may have had 'carer' and 'participation' in the title but were medically oriented pieces. 'Involvement' was principally of a clinical or technical nature, papers where involvement was a means to a specific clinical end and where carers' lives and voices were not the focus of the study.

The abstracts obtained were then reviewed by two members of the research team in relation to the inclusion criteria and agreed decisions made on whether to obtain a hard copy of the full article. Where possible, these articles were downloaded or accessed through journals held by the University of Sunderland. Where material was not directly available, as much as possible was accessed via the British Library inter-library loan service. Articles were then analysed using the article summary sheet (*see* Appendix F).

All articles were selected using a seconding approach that triaged those publications and reports that had carer participation, inclusion or involvement as their focus. Where article content was unclear, further investigation or actual acquisition of a document was undertaken. Articles have been double read for meaning and for fit with the literature review.

Following the analysis of abstracts and articles obtained, 101 articles were identified as relevant to the research.

2.2 Country and coverage specified

The majority of the research has been carried out in England with a few articles featuring research in or about carers in Northern Ireland. There were few articles in Wales, and what there was were official reports. More research was available in a Scottish context, but due to the Position Paper's focus, only a small number were selected.

2.3 Focus of the review

The overall focus of research has varied widely, covering a broad range of topics in relation to carers – from carer assessments and discharge planning to the use of technology and involvement in job interviews. Many obviously focused on specific care recipient groups, of which the one that appears most frequently is older people with mental health problems, particularly in relation to dementia.

2.4 Types of carers

One of the important aspects of this research is to try and identify the particular needs of different kinds of carers, particularly marginalised carer groupings such as BME carers and gay and lesbian carers. However, a reading of the research material suggests that, generally, carers are regarded as an undifferentiated grouping.

In the vast majority of the articles, the only information given to differentiate between carers is in terms of the gender balance and age of the sample. In only seven cases was there any mention of their ethnic background. One of these articles focused specifically on Asian carers and the other six mentioned that some of the carers were from BME backgrounds.

In relation to another not very visible group, only one article focused specifically on older carers. And only one mentioned the sexual orientation or identity of the carers or commented on it as an issue.

2.5 Types of people cared for

A wide variety of service users were mentioned in the literature. Sometimes the type of service user was not specified as this did not relate to the topic of the research. Again the two most common user groups were older people with dementia and older people with mental health problems.

2.6 Types of knowledge

Following the SCIE Knowledge review conventions, the types of knowledge used in each article or report surveyed was noted. This Position Paper has been guided by the Department of Health's (DH's) *Quality strategy for social care* (2000), SCIE conventions and recent appraisals of the need to value knowledge diversity (151). 'Knowledge' was understood in terms of the following categories:

Conceptual knowledge Knowledge that explores the meanings of participation, power sharing or empowerment for carers: references 22, 81, 102, 152, 163, 181, 182, 188, 215.

Empirical knowledge Knowledge that is based on a piece of primary and/or secondary research on carer participation, carer–professional interactions, support for carers, 'hidden' carers' experiences: references 65, 120, 153, 155, 158, 162, 165, 170, 171, 176, 179, 183, 184, 185, 186, 187, 189, 190, 193, 196, 197, 198, 200, 202, 203, 204, 205, 206, 207, 208, 211, 214, 219, 224, 225, 227, 228, 230, 233, 234, 235, 236, 237, 238, 240, 241, 242, 243, 244, 246.

Descriptive knowledge Knowledge that conveys key carer data without systematic analysis. This includes major reports and policy guidance on carer roles and stresses that help inform debates about the need for greater carer participation. Secondary data is often provided in such knowledge sources: references 154, 164, 167, 168, 191, 192, 199, 207, 209, 210, 212, 229.

A number of articles contained both conceptual and empirical knowledge: 11, 67, 75, 159, 160, 161, 166, 169, 173, 178, 179, 195, 210, 213, 216, 218, 226, 231, 232.

2.7 Types of research

The great majority of the research is qualitative in its approach with very few quantitative studies. A small number of the studies examined could be described as evaluative as the researchers sought to evaluate a new service, project or scheme.

2.8 Review sample

Except for the few purely theoretical studies that are used to provide a framework for key ideas and principles in carer participation and a small number of descriptive studies, all the articles report on research where there has been direct contact with carers. In some cases, service users and professional staff have also been involved in the research project, but they have not been the focus of this review.

2.9 Carer participation studies: a profile of methods

As the majority of the research studies reported on have used a qualitative approach, it is not surprising that the most common research method has been interviewing. In addition, 28 studies used mixed methods, which included – as well as structured and semi-structured interviews – focus groups, documentary analysis and participant observation (references 51, 67, 120, 153, 155, 167, 169, 170, 171, 173, 176, 179, 190,

198, 202, 205, 207, 208, 223, 225, 226, 228, 230, 231, 235, 236, 238, 243). The majority of the interviews have been face-to-face but on a few occasions telephone interviewing has been used.

A significant number of studies involved researching both carers and users (n=16) (references 65, 67, 116, 160, 173, 178, 187, 193, 197, 203, 213, 214, 216, 223, 225, 235). An even greater number of studies involved researching both carers and professionals (n=23) (references 51, 65, 68, 155, 159, 166, 167, 173, 176, 179, 193, 197, 198, 202, 205, 217, 219, 223, 226, 230, 231, 235, 236).

3 Carer participation: published studies

The literature reviewed for this study reveals a considerable diversity of levels of carer participation and involvement. It also presents a wide range of carers and types of users cared for. As the research aimed to map the literature of carer participation and to examine the breadth of literature available, as well as identify the gaps, this diversity is not surprising. As there were clearly no theoretical approaches or specific model or technique that could organise the literature, it was decided to use an overall framework for thinking about participation as a guiding principle, one that draws on an amalgam of helpful conceptualisations of carer participation. For example, Arnstein's 1969 model of a 'ladder of participation', which was developed in the context of citizen involvement in planning processes in the United States, describes eight steps that go from *non-participation* (manipulation and therapy), through degrees of *tokenism* (informing, consultation and placation) to degrees of *citizen power* (partnership, delegated power and citizen control) (152).

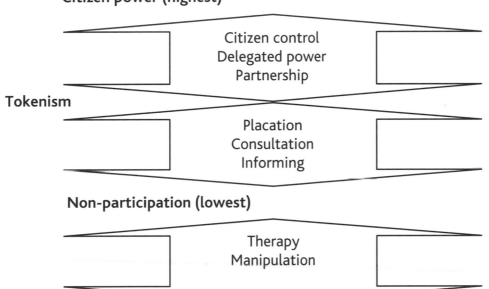

Citizen power (highest)

Citizen control
Delegated power
Partnership

Tokenism

Placation
Consultation
Informing

Non-participation (lowest)

Therapy
Manipulation

In the field of partnership nursing, Casey (153) identifies a typology of nurses' partnership with informal carers in a medical setting, noting a continuum from *exclusion* to *permission* to *assumption* to *negotiation*. Casey's research is a synthesis of earlier (largely pre-1993) studies of nurse and carer interactions. Negotiation was a professional stance where skilled paediatric staff were willing to negotiate options and make minimal assumptions about treatment and discharge processes. What is less clear from Casey is why certain therapeutic environments are more likely to offer negotiated approaches to parental carers.

Goss and Miller (81), when looking at different relationships between user/carers and staff in planning and developing services, talk about five types of relationships: *no involvement, consumer education, limited two-way communication, listening and response, partnership*. The Audit Commission (154) describe a continuum from *individual consultation* to *participation in planning* to *user/carer-led control and management*.

It was felt that the material uncovered by the literature review fell into three categories:

* **Consultation:** where the views of carers, either as individuals or in groups, have been sought on a variety of topics or services. In these cases, either no feedback has been given to the carers involved or it is unclear whether the carers have been informed of any outcomes.
* **Consultation with feedback or exploration of outcomes:** the views of carers have been sought and they have been given feedback on the outcome of the study or the impact on services.
* **Participation:** carers, either as individuals, representatives or groups, have participated in the planning of the activity or process under investigation.

These three categories are discussed below. Separate sections deal with articles focused on black and minority ethnic carers and on lesbian and gay carers.

3.1 Consultation

A considerable number of studies fell into the category of a consultation process where carers were asked their views on a variety of topics, from a general exploration of carers' needs, including information (references 51, 65, 116, 160, 162, 164, 168, 178, 185, 186, 188, 206, 207, 208, 210, 221, 233), to their views of specific services – for example, respite care (references 183, 204, 225, 226).

A number of studies focused on carer support and discharge services (references 187, 189, 193, 196, 201, 203, 240, 242), carer expense payments (reference 146), balancing carer/paid worker issues (references 228, 229) and carers' views of the operation and effects of the Carers (Recognition and Services) Act 1995 and carer assessments (references 67, 68, 111, 173, 230).

Studies that involved consultation with family carers about the effectiveness of the Carers (Recognition and Services) Act 1995 have established the gap between rhetoric and delivery of assessment and, therefore, support for carers who otherwise make substantial commitments to caring for others (230). In 2001, following Henwood's 1998 report Ignored and invisible (37) for the Carers National Association (now Carers UK), the Association performed a follow-up study to reflect on the impact of the *Caring for carers* strategy on hospital discharge practices. The number of carers consulted on hospital discharge had actually fallen from 71% to 64% between 1998 and 2001 (85). Other Carers National Association research, while not studies of consultation and participation *per se*, are worthy of mention as they are large-scale studies and point to the continued participation deficits in the key areas of carer policy and practice/emergency care planning (241). Similar deficits were identified in a survey of the responses of LDPBs to the *Valuing people* document on meeting the needs of older family carers (242).

One article from the Royal College of Psychiatrists (227) involved consultation with carers of people with mental health problems, with the aim of developing more appropriate tools to assess carer needs. This was felt to be important given the greater role played by clinical assessors using a care programme approach (CPA) in assessing user and carer needs in mental health contexts. The need to be aware of social as well as clinical needs was acknowledged in this research. However, as with much consultation work, it is unclear what the tangible outcomes will be for carers.

Consultation articles also addressed the potential of carers' input in enhancing professional education (153, 216) and training of professionals and/or carers (65, 213, 214, 216). A study by Preston-Shoot (223) points to the significance of mismatches between the perceptions of social workers, users and carers of needs across a range of services and supports (day care, respite care, emergency planning, social and emotional needs, ability to continue caring). There is much evidence in this study that statutory services have some distance to travel in apprehending carers' complex and often shifting needs. Kersten (65) interviewed 64 carers (alongside the 'severely disabled' people they cared for) and established that professionals and service users underestimated the need for carers' short breaks compared to carers' own perceptions.

Pickard, Jacobs and Kirk (231) undertook a broad-ranging study of carers of older people and of technology-dependent children and paid carers (beyond the scope of this review). They established that informal carer groups (they use the term 'lay carers') were involved in a range of often clinically intrusive and technical procedures and that these roles and tasks were often not open to carers' negotiation. Pickard suggests that not only should decision-making processes be critically reflected on by professionals, who should also make fewer assumptions about carer openness to undertake clinical procedures, but also that carer expertise in caring should be more fully acknowledged. The latter would help shift the power balance in the lay/ professional relationship.

Rethink undertook wide-ranging research (233) on carer involvement, information, services and support some four years after the advent of the NSF for mental health (Department of Health, 1999). Although some improvement had been made in levels of involvement, there was significant regional variation in the levels of involvement in information sharing and service influence. As one carer put it: "You have to pester to improve conditions".

In these studies, the care recipients covered the vast majority of types of service users, including older people and those with mental health problems, learning disabilities, terminal illness and/or dementia. In most cases, the types of carers are not specified, except in relation to the age and gender of the sample. Only 10 studies relate to a particular type of carer – older carers (162) and Asian carers (22, 120, 160, 176, 190, 200, 211, 244, 248). However, if we look at studies that are exclusively about black and Asian carers, the figure falls to four (120, 191, 203, 244). Black carers are themselves diverse, of course, as the study by the Welsh Assembly noted in including spousal carers, adult carers, older carers and so on (121). A study by Scott, Whyler and Grant (168) noted the diverse constituency and needs of carers according to gender, age and length of caring experience.

One key factor in carer diversity is the paid work commitments of carers. There is a growing literature on worker carers that highlights the need for employer awareness and flexibility and the need for statutory support to help carers juggle their paid work and informal caring commitments. Enhanced links between social care organisations and employers were important, as was the avoidance of *a priori* assumptions about worker carers' likely care commitments (228, 229). Research by Yeandle, Crompton, Wigfield and Dennet (236) points to the low levels of employer flexibility as regards carer employees, and the importance of locality in the provision of wider family support. For example, family support for worker carers was higher among those carers consulted in the Sheffield area compared to Kent carers where greater social mobility had erased the broader informal social support networks.

Not surprisingly, given the topic of the review and the search questions used, the vast majority of the studies used a qualitative approach in their research, with only five studies making significant use of quantitative methods employing self-completed questionnaires (20, 207, 208, 233, 241). An additional eight studies researched more than 100 (and fewer than 1,000) carers (51, 153, 172, 187, 189, 203, 227, 244). The main research method used in the qualitative studies was the interview, generally on a face-to-face basis, although some studies included telephone interviews, focus groups (213), involvement protocol and tool testing (219, 227). The sample sizes of carers involved in the studies varied greatly – from three (160) through to a Princess Royal Trust survey of 3,000 carers (207) to major studies by Carers UK involving a survey of 10,000 carers' views on key carer legislation on access to support and service involvement (208). Some studies used a mixture of methods – for example, Casey's study (153) of partnership nursing and carer involvement in a paediatric nursing setting used structured interviews (n=243), secondary documented clinical notes and ethnographic methods. A number of the studies (51, 160, 162, 175) included interviews with users as well as with carers, and in some others (68, 173), professionals' views were also included. However, the focus in this review is on carers' views.

The *Carers speak out* project (207) carried out in 2002 by the Princess Royal Trust aimed to consult carers about their needs, priorities and issues. Consultation meetings with more than 1,000 carers and professionals were held throughout the UK and in excess of 2,800 questionnaires were completed by carers. The project identified that carers needed access to good sources of information, help and support. However, the situation had improved over the previous five years for newer carers. The survey also revealed concerns about the number and quality of carer assessments, with some areas of the UK showing a reduction in the number carried out. There were regional variations, with Wales and the south of England having a higher proportion of surveyed carers who had received an assessment. Only half of those assessed said the process led to extra services. Research by Rummery, Ellis and Davis (67) for the Joseph Rowntree Foundation, which consisted of 23 carer interviews, similarly suggests that – despite national assessment guidance – LA contexts and differential social worker interpretations of the guidance led to diverse interpretations that disadvantaged some carers. Despite the Carers (Recognition and Services) Act 1995, there was little evidence that carers were routinely informed of their legal entitlement to a full assessment (67). Research by Manthorpe and Twigg (232) highlights the street-level challenges and contradictions between the philosophy of care management, managerialism and carer involvement.

While these studies are not focusing on specific issues of carer participation *per se*, their findings do offer some information on particular barriers and issues in relation to a number of different areas of carer involvement. Those that focus on carers' views of service provision (51, 168, 173, 178, 183, 185, 187, 196, 204) identify such things as the need to provide carers with more information on user illnesses (sometimes the nature of an illness or 'condition', but more often in relation to the specific effects on the person being cared for), the problems of matching carer choice with the resources available, the need for better access to specialist services such as palliative care, and the need for more information and support in dealing with medication. Beck and Minghella's study (196), which involved 78 carers and concerned a service to support carers generally, identified that they wanted better access to services, 24-hour support and more practical support such as respite care. A meta-study by Harding and Higginson (234) looked at the interventions in home-based palliative care most likely to dovetail with carers' needs and self-perceptions.

Two studies on carers' views on respite care (183, 204) report on carer satisfaction with respite because it offers carers 'normality' and 'freedom' but, at the same time, enables care recipients to stay in the community longer than might otherwise be possible. The availability of social supports around carers is also identified as increasing carer satisfaction with respite.

In a research report for the NHS Service Delivery and Organisation RandD Programme (205), the Social Policy Research Unit examined the effectiveness of support services for carers of people with mental health problems. The researchers consulted with 19 key informant carers (as well as other stakeholders) and, among other findings, identified the need for more research in relation to BME carers and those caring in a same-sex relationship.

A study on how LAs have implemented the Carers (Recognition and Services) Act 1995 (68) revealed carers' limited understanding of the Act, with a particular lack of clarity about the purpose of assessment. Carers felt that there was limited concern about their own needs. and that there was a focus on carers' ability to continue caring rather than on whether they wanted to do so. A report (202) that looks at carers' access to healthcare identifies five types of barriers: professional characteristics; service issues; language or cultural issues; care or care recipient characteristics; and information and knowledge issues. These issues cover such common areas as: professionals focusing on care recipients at the expense of carers; the way service systems are organised; and language barriers and racial stereotyping. Problems were also identified as resulting from the fact that many carers do not identify themselves as carers, and from lack of access to information, sometimes exacerbated by professional confidentiality issues.

Similar findings are evident in a study of 'partnership nursing' and the involvement of parent carers in a paediatric health setting (153). However, nursing styles and 'nursing-centred' professional culture were seen as the primary factor in limiting parent/carer partnership. The study concludes that this professional dominance is less likely in a domestic caring setting, but sadly, the evidence from community nursing does not bear this out. A study (214) of service users' and carers' views on community mental health nurses (CMHNs) suggests that carers feel that they are least likely to be kept informed and involved in the overall planning and delivery of care and support.

A focus group study of user and carer input into learning disability nurse education and training (213) notes the limited and unsystematic involvement of users and carers, where even consultation was limited. The study suggests that learning difficulty nurses and their professional organisations could do much more to convert the ideas present in *Valuing people* (90) into reality. Most studies of carer involvement in education and training focus on the field of health and medicine. However, one study has begun the process of reflecting on carers' contribution to social work training (215). Manthorpe's work is not based on primary research and is not, strictly speaking, a study of consultation; rather, it is an exploration of how best to involve carers in social work training. This study is useful, however, as it raises issues of carer diversity and the need to go beyond single carer testimony in highlighting carer needs to trainee social workers (216).

A growing number of articles consider how best to enhance carer participation and support. However, such work needs to be tested with primary research and, where successful professional models are identified, implemented (224). However, more creative examples are emerging in the literature that do involve carers directly. An action research project in Scotland (based on English pilot studies) looked at the impact of a carer development worker post on dialogue between health and social services and carers. Although the development worker was able to highlight the needs of carers more fully, the feedback from carers was that consultation is limited, particularly as regards information needs (237). Another Scottish study is applicable as it looked at the efficacy of UK-wide professional guidelines on dementia. The study, which consulted carers of people with dementia about the value and fitness of the guidelines, found that, while essentially sound, they failed to take carer narratives and ground-level expertise into account. Plans are in place to alter these guidelines in the future, although no time scales or continued carer involvement is cited (238).

While these studies have consulted directly with carers on their views, the lack of follow-up or focus on outcomes limits their value in relation to carer participation issues. However, they do identify what carers see as barriers and restrictions on the understanding of, and involvement in, services. These factors include lack of information, lack of resources, problems with access to services and the need for more effective monitoring and review.

A number of studies were concerned exclusively with conceptual and theoretical constructions of caring and informal care, its interface with formal care structures. Most of these articles argue for more critical reflection on how care is constructed as this will help contextualise how and why partnership working takes place (11, 22, 102, 158, 163, 181, 182). Some papers or reports synthesised available best practice in carer participation both as systematic reviews and more focused reports or literature reviews (164, 184, 199, 248).

3.2 Consultation with feedback or exploration of outcomes

Relatively few of the studies include any follow-up or focus on outcomes (references 155, 161, 169, 171, 172, 176, 179, 191, 200, 219, 222, 243, 245). For those that do include follow-up, the time period for this varies between six months and two years. For the report by Wenger, Scott and Seddon (161), based on the carer component of the larger Gwynedd Dementia Study, a proportion of carers were reinterviewed after two years on the experience of caring for older people with dementia in a rural area. These findings revealed that, although carers received a relatively low level of service, they still expressed satisfaction with what they did receive. A comparative study (172) that evaluated outcomes for (a) carers receiving a specialist mental health service that focuses on carers directly and (b) standard mental health services aimed at care recipients with dementia reinterviewed participants after eight months. It reports no significant differences between the two groups and suggests that the outcome for care recipients is no worse when there is a carer focus and that there is some benefit to carers in having support directed towards them.

The Social Policy Research Unit at York has carried out a range of research into carers and carer involvement. Its research (179) into the Carers Act 1995 looked at the impact of carer assessments from the carer's perspective in four English LA/SSDs (as well as interviewing managers and practitioners). The research methodology involved the assessment of 51 carers of older people and included follow-up interviews with carers six months after the initial contact. Carers noted the validating experience of having their views about caring taken into account and appreciated the support services received. The need to respond to the issue of emotional support was identified, and follow-up interviews showed that many carers did not receive any feedback from their assessment and were not clear what they might have expected to have resulted from it. In a later article (180), Arksey discusses the research findings in terms of a rationing process and, in particular, a self-rationing response by carers who do not expect that services or resources will be available. (*See also* reference, 200.)

In their research into carer assessments, Robinson and Williams (155) carried out follow-up interviews a year after the original assessment in order to look specifically at outcomes in terms of user satisfaction. They report that, while carers appreciated the assessment for its own sake as recognising their role as carers, in practical terms only 18 of 42 services discussed had been provided to the whole sample. They conclude their paper by stating:

> Carers' needs assessments are still a very minor feature in the lives of those supporting people with learning disabilities. They are rarely offered and delivered, and even more rarely acted upon.

Three papers describe group processes involving carers. Two of these, which look at carer support groups (176) and a training course (169), use a variety of methods for gathering information prior to the research and for post-intervention assessment. The third paper (191) discusses the use of a consensus group made up of carers to consult on Health Advisory Service standards for evaluation of mental health services for older people. The proposals and amendments from the carers were then incorporated into the final set of standards. A number of articles draw together wider evidence in exhorting professionals to involve carers more fully in service planning. One example is Took (245), whose conceptual work on the meaning and value of involving users and carers in the mental health field draws on work completed by the National Schizophrenia Fellowship (now Rethink). Took represents a good example of how service improvement can be aided by drawing on the expertise of carers and users and giving feedback to them.

A study by Rogers (243) presents an action research project that involved general practitioners (GPs) and carers of people with dementia and mental health problems. Using a structured questionnaire (Stage 1), this three-stage study identified gaps in current carer support. Key issues were the length of time taken between GP and consultant involvement with mental health carers and users, and the lack of information for carers on how to support the people that they are caring for. Stages 2 and 3 took the form of carer focus groups to explore these barriers further and work with carers and professionals to begin to plug the gap between current provision and carers' stated needs.

A 'carer-led' study of the potential future role of multimedia programme resources to enhance information and knowledge of respite care services involved carers in using telematic interventions as an exploratory research approach to enhancing carer options in accessing respite care. This study illustrates the possible role of information and communications technology (ICT) in making enhanced respite choices available. However, the study only used four family carers in the user trials, and the exact involvement of carers in framing the trial parameters is not clear (219).

The papers that discuss work that includes follow-up with carers and a focus on carer outcomes cover a wide range of research, from narrative accounts to comparative studies using specific quantitative measurements. There are, again, limitations of sample size and research methodology, and only a few studies can identify specific positive or negative outcomes for carers.

3.3 Participation

Literature in which carers themselves participate in the development of services (159, 165, 166, 167, 170, 174, 192, 197), training (217) and research (218) is limited. This includes direct carer involvement in the development and testing of new technology to provide information for and to support carers in the home (165); and also, in Simpson's study (170), of records held by carers in the home to assess their role as partners with professionals in the planning of care. Both were pilot studies that involved carers in the on-going evaluation of the tools and their effectiveness as part of the development process. However, carers were not involved in the original discussions and planning and were being asked to evaluate specific information tools rather than the overall importance of such tools to the carer role as a whole. It is worth noting that a quarter of the sample in the Simpson study did not find the process of holding care records valuable.

Walker and Dewar (159) looked specifically at ways of facilitating carer involvement in decision making and, drawing on the views of carers, identified four markers of satisfactory involvement: (a) feeling that information is being shared; (b) feeling you are being included in decision-making; (c) feeling that there is someone you can contact when you need to; and (d) feeling that the service is responsive to your needs. The research showed that the majority of carers were dissatisfied with their level of involvement.

The study also looked at ways of improving carer involvement by working with hospital staff to encourage them to be more proactive in engaging with carers. It did this by developing some guidelines for improving involvement, and suggested a series of questions that could be used to promote better carer involvement. In a later article, Dewar, Tocher and Watson (166) tested the implementation of these guidelines within a hospital setting.

Other articles present a more comprehensive approach to carer participation where carers are involved from the beginning in the design and implementation of the project. Nicholas (174) presents the findings of a developmental project that was part of the Department of Health *Health outcomes* programme, and which included carer collaboration via a carer reference group and involvement with an Asian carers' group. This work uses a focus on carer-identified outcomes as a guiding principle at all stages of the project, from initial assessment to review. It also utilises a number of self-assessment documents as tools to facilitate flexible interactions between carers and practitioners.

Some governmental research presents findings that encompass examples of participation (still limited) and consultation (now widespread). A recent SSI study of LA responses to the 'Modernisation Agenda' noted that much progress is being made in the structures of involvement, but that substantive carer outcomes are still notable by their scarcity (228). Barr, Stenhouse and Henderson undertook an action research project based on an evaluation of the impact of a social inclusion policy for Asian carers in four Scottish localities (190).

A participatory research study by Carpenter and Sbaraini (197) into the CPA involved carers (and users) in the design and evaluation of the project, and as interviewers as part of an advisory group. Of the 28 carers interviewed, the great majority said they wanted to be more involved in the care of their relative. While many of the carers felt that professionals encouraged them to express their views, a sizeable proportion reported that their views were not actually being taken into account. Again, there were problems about being given information, and a majority felt that this process was inadequate. However, where the person cared for was involved in a care programme, these problems were less evident.

A good example of interprofessional working in the direct involvement of carers was found in the study carried out by Turner, Sheldon, Coles, Mountford, Hillier, Radawy and Wee (217). They used family carers' voices in palliative care workshops in the training of medical, nursing and social work professionals. This involvement of carers was based on interviews, but shared decision making and participation were guiding principles of the research and wider training.

One particularly instructive article (218) focused on direct participation in research and comprised three parent carer research projects (related to carers) that provided some wider insights into the value of consulting carers to enhance both carer research and the lives of carers. The article, the lead author of which is himself a parent carer, suggests that, while carer involvement and consultation is beneficial, the following are prerequisites of more complete involvement:

- Time needs to be built into a project so that the complexities and practicalities of carer involvement are fully accounted for.
- Consideration should be given to the physical, social and emotional needs of participants.
- Participants need to be kept informed throughout the research project.

This article raises issues of emancipatory or participatory research more generally, an issue that is discussed in the practice survey (*see* Section 5).

Other articles (167, 192) have a more practice-based focus and describe specific examples of carer participation. One of these is a joint initiative to develop an integrated service strategy and implementation strategy plan for older people's mental health services (192). However, this project only involved the carer representative on a development group. A second project involved carers (and users) in the appointment of a manager for the learning disability services of a PCT. Prior to the interviews for the post, the carers participated in a training programme and in the development of questions to ask the candidates. The structure of each interview was altered to facilitate the involvement of the carers and users, and it was agreed by the PCT chief executive that no one would be appointed if they were considered inappropriate by the carer/user representatives.

One of the important findings of this material is that carer participation is dependent on the abilities and actions of the practitioners and professionals involved. The research also shows that carers appreciate services that recognise their expertise, treat them as individuals, and facilitate accessibility and responsiveness to changing needs, and where staff are proactive and work to develop positive relationships with carers.

3.4 BME carers

It is striking that the great majority of the formal research literature examined in this review makes no mention of BME carers, either in discussions of the research sample or in the conclusions of the research. Eighteen articles (22, 67, 120, 155, 160, 174, 176, 182, 187, 190, 200, 203, 204, 207, 209, 211, 222, 246) explicitly mention that BME carers were the focus (*n*=8) or were included in the research sample (*n*=8) and even fewer comment on whether there were any differences between the responses of these carers and white carers (203). This is changing somewhat in more recent research reports and in documents produced by carers' organisations and specifically black carers' organisations.

Building on work done in the project *Carers' needs and the Carers Act* (62), which recommended that further research should look at ways to reach BME carers and promote access to carer assessment, Hepworth (200) explored ways to counteract the apparent social exclusion of such carers from care planning processes. Consultative workshops were held with voluntary organisations and carer representatives, and some of the outcomes were that BME carers need appropriate information and guidance to access services and that, as well as sensitivity to cultural issues, carers felt that getting access to mainstream services was very important.

Another study tested carer assessment tools – CADI (Carers' Assessment of Difficulties Index) and CASI (Carers' Assessment of Satisfactions Index), developed by Nolan, Grant and Keady (102) – to see if they could be used appropriately with BME carers. They are supposed to assess both the stress and satisfaction of caring from a carer's perspective. The tools were made available in different languages (English, Urdu and Gujarati) and the interviews were supported by first-language support workers. From the Asian carers' point of view, the tools were useful and did not need to be amended. Some key findings were that their satisfaction in caring related to a sense of family duty and religious faith, and that the minority ethnic support groups to which they belonged were very important.

A report by Forbat and Nar (246) looks at the difficulties that African/Caribbean and South Asian carers of family members with dementia had in accessing services. The research found that the carers were often isolated and, for various reasons, received little help from their families, a finding that challenges the common notion that such families wish to 'look after their own'. The need to challenge this notion has been emphasised by the 1999 DH/SSI report (211), which stated that:

> The inaccurate assumption that 'they look after their own' has to be challenged by those with responsibility for developing services because this is often used to justify inadequate provision or low take-up.

This assumption is directly reflected in the title of the report by WAG into the accessibility of carers' services to BME carers in Wales: *Challenging the myth: 'They look after their own'* (120). Although the actual number involved was relatively small – 43 carers – there was a diversity of ethnicity and carer category. The project also consulted LAs, voluntary organisations and community groups (four of which were black-led). It is worth noting that the consultation with community groups helped identify people in those communities who were caring for family members but who did not see themselves as carers.

Some of the issues raised by these BME carers as barriers to access to care services echo those mentioned by carers more generally: not being clear about what an assessment is, not knowing whether they have been assessed or not and not having information on what services could be provided. However, these barriers are exacerbated by existing services not being provided in a culturally sensitive manner, which may make them unacceptable to the carers. The WAG report emphasises the importance of effective communication and the availability of language-matched information and interpretation. BME carers can also be isolated by a lack of English language skills, which can then lead to service providers stereotyping carers as wanting to 'look after their own'. However, the report makes clear that BME carers would welcome supportive services if they were offered in a culturally sensitive manner.

A report (22) from the Joseph Rowntree Foundation on BME parents carers who are looking after severely disabled children identified many similar issues restricting access to services. It noted that South Asian and black African/Caribbean families reported levels of support from their extended families that were less than those found among white families in similar circumstances. In particular, the support from partners for mothers in all ethnic groups was less than that reported by white mothers. As for the problems in accessing services, all ethnic groups reported a lack of information, delays in services and having to 'fight' for services, and many families also had low expectations of support. Barr, Stenhouse and Henderson (190) present findings of a cluster (*n*=4) of action research projects that included a South Asian carers project that aimed to provide social support to empower carers of disabled children. While greater social partnership is still some distance away, the direct involvement of professionals and carers/users was seen to further the social inclusion agenda. A report (211) by the SSI on LA work with BME carers backs up this message.

While not a research report as such, a good practice guide (209) for people working with black carers, produced by the Afiya Trust and the National Black Carers Workers Network, has many useful pointers towards good practice with black carers. Written by black workers, it draws on their knowledge and experience. The guide emphasises many of the difficulties experienced by black carers in accessing information and services that have been mentioned above, and also highlights the social exclusion experienced because of unemployment or low-paid work, poor housing and poverty, all of which puts extra pressure on black carers. However, it then goes on to focus on examples of good practice and proposes checklists to guide workers and organisations towards more culturally appropriate and effective support for black carers.

3.5 Lesbian, gay and bisexual carers

While there is limited material, particularly in the traditional research literature, on specific issues affecting BME carers, the literature review revealed that gay and lesbian carers have been more or less completely ignored. Only one article by Manthorpe (203) addresses the issue directly and it is mainly a theoretical discussion about the neglect of any consideration of issues of caring within lesbian couples. It identifies two areas of neglect:

> ... a neglect in conceptualisation of caring that carers may not be heterosexual and that lesbian carers may have needs and strengths linked to their sexual orientation whether caring for 'partners' or members of their families.

This article notes that, because of homophobic attitudes, some lesbians may choose to not reveal their sexuality but to pass as heterosexual with their own and/or with their partner's families or with professionals. Manthorpe summarises the issues involved for lesbian carers when caring for a partner as: issues around rights in a care or medical setting; inheritance and succession rights; acceptance by others, particularly kin; and involvement and recognition by professionals.

It appears to be mainly within carer and voluntary organisations that issues in relation to lesbian, gay, bisexual and transgender (LGBT) carers are being discussed and addressed. The Alzheimer's Society Lesbian and Gay Network, which has been in existence for over six years, aims to provide information about the support offered by the society and to work towards improving and making services appropriate for lesbian and gay carers. It does this via a regular newsletter, by supporting local organisations around the country and by addressing staff training and awareness of LGBT issues. It is also noteworthy that some of the earliest efforts to engage with LGBT carers came out of Age Concern carer work.

A best practice guide on health care for LGB service users and their carers has recently been produced by the public services union Unison and the Royal College of Nursing (212). It notes the extra barriers that these service users and carers experience in accessing services as it is often not safe for same-sex partners to be open about their sexuality. They fear that staff may assume that they are heterosexual or may be hostile to them if they reveal their sexuality. There are specific issues for LGBT carers in terms of being informed about treatment and other issues in relation to the person for whom they are caring, and often the term 'next of kin' is used in a way that excludes carers.

3.6 Gaps in the literature

The above has outlined those areas that have received attention in the literature. There are, however, a number of gaps that need to be identified at this stage. The following received little or no attention and yet are clearly pertinent to any understanding of carer participation:

Under-represented

- Studies of the quantified effect of carer participation, both in terms of service and carer impact.
- Studies that look at current methods or tools for evaluating carer impact and their effectiveness.
- Studies that delineate by 'carer group' the various ways of understanding meaningful carer involvement.
- Explorations, both empirical and conceptual, of those factors that mediate between strategic and 'street-level' carer involvement and impact.
- Studies of what works to increase previously 'hidden' carers' involvement.

Not currently reflected in the literature

- Understanding the 'expert carer' phenomenon – a boon or a barrier?
- Barriers faced by carers of those with substance abuse/misuse.
- Older gay and lesbian carers.

4 Carer participation: illustrative examples from the grey literature

This section of the Position Paper shows examples of projects or services that suggest degrees of carer participation and involvement. They are taken from the SIGLE (System for Information on Grey Literature in Europe) unpublished (grey) literature electronic database and from a systematic trawl of statutory and voluntary sector websites.

There were many thousands of references to carer participation in the grey literature. As this Position Paper is primarily looking at best practice, the research team has attempted to categorise examples into the same framework as used for the literature review. This is based on an amalgam of ideas derived from Arnstein's 'Ladder of participation' (152) and Goss and Miller's typology of relationships between users, carers and staff in planning and delivering services (81). The categories used are those that suggest carers are involved at a level of:

* consultation
* consultation with feedback or exploration of outcomes
* participation.

Relevant grey literature was also requested from organisations taking part in the telephone interviews for the practice survey. Information was less forthcoming from this source, understandably when busy people had already given of their time by filling in questionnaires and giving telephone interviews. However, the examples show the range and sometimes the depth of carer involvement in the statutory and/ or voluntary sectors. The most exciting ones manage to bring together carers, carer organisations and the statutory sector in an alliance to enhance the lives of carers.

The illustrative examples are taken mainly from unpublished reports, public information documents and organisations' strategies and reviews. They are not peer-reviewed for content, currency or accuracy, and they are uncorroborated. However, they do illustrate the efforts that organisations are making. Organisations are named because the material is already public, or has been passed to the research team with the agreement that their names can be made public. When only basic web addresses are given, this means that the best route to the relevant part of the carer site is via the general address and the site's search facility.

4.1 Consultation

Age Concern Suffolk's 'Younger People with Dementia' (YPWD) Project
established a single point of contact for service users, carers and families, alongside partnership links with clinical specialists and wider support groups. Partnership working is seen to involve all key stakeholders within a philosophy of considering both carer and cared for as equal partners. The project has established a log of evidence of experiences of dementia services and shortfalls in provision. Carers are a key voice in these activities.
www.alzheimers.org.uk/Research/Library/reading_lists/Readinglist_YPWD.pdf

Rethink's Birmingham African Caribbean Carers Development Service provides carer support to BME carers supporting those with mental health problems in the Birmingham area. As well as direct carer support, the project works with other carer agencies to raise awareness of mental health issues and the needs of carers. Similar development work is also taking place in Gravesend and Bristol Rethink BME carers services.

www.rethink.org/how_we_can_help/our_services/west_midlands/birmingham_
afric.html

Caerphilly Carers Strategy Group (Caerphilly Social Services/Caerphilly County Borough Council) has brought carers together with service providers via a well-publicised Carers' Week and Carers' Day (for leisure access). Carers' voices are heard through the roll out of a number of carers groups, and a carers' website has also been established to alert carers to the latest information.

www.wales.gov.uk/subicarersnew/content/carers_secondary_analysis-e.doc

The Community Care Needs Assessment Project (CCNAP) has formulated guidance on how best to involve users and carers. The guidance provides conceptual and practical advice on how local health and social care authorities should respond to policy and practice imperatives. The guide provides some examples of user and carer involvement work currently under way.

www.ccnap.org.uk/Guide/part1.htm

Hampshire County Council has established rigorous performance indicators to improve carers' services, which include carer involvement. For example, it aims to develop an electronic database of carer information (to include a target for hard-to-reach carers in new care contracts), to extend outreach work with BME carers and to consult on whether or not to extend direct payments.

www.hants.gov.uk/TC/bestval/plans/carers&respitecare.html

Kent County Council has fostered a scheme called 'Partnership with parents', which works closely with schools across Kent to help parents (including parent carers) to access information, services and involvement in children's services. The 'Partnership' scheme is seen to help parents by engaging them more fully in educational and support issues, while aiding schools' understanding of parents' needs.

www.kent.gov.uk/education-and-learning/special-and-additional-education/
partnership-with-parents/

Fareham and Gosport Rethink Carers Group have worked with professionals in acute mental health admissions settings. The project involved a named member of staff providing carers with a leaflet containing information on a local carers group and how to make contact with it. On discharge, contact with the local carers group is once again facilitated.

www.rethink.org
www.hants.gov.uk/socservs/domcare/carers.html

Bury Metropolitan Borough Council has striven hard to commission services that have explicit reference to 'hidden' carers in their brief and aims to enhance the access of service users and carers to services. More specific measures include a day centre proving support and information to carers of disabled children and adults within the local Asian and Jewish communities. Bury have used *Quality protects* monies strategically to improve access to services for children, young people and their carers.

www.bury.gov.uk

The Parkinson's Disease Society in collaboration with the **Multiple Sclerosis (MS) Society** have developed a 'BME Carer Outreach' project to involve these carers more fully in influencing service and quality for carers of those with neurological impairments. The MS Society report *Caring counts* (2004) and the 2003 MS Society's 'Carers Programme' extends commitment to this and to the profile of carers more generally.

www.parkinsons.org.uk
www.mssociety.org.uk/life_with_ms/carers/index.html

As part of the 2005 Carers Week, the **MS Society, Carers** UK, **Crossroads: Caring for Carers**, the **Princess Royal Trust for Carers, Rethink, Macmillan Cancer Relief** and **Help the Aged** have formed an alliance, with a particular and timely focus on the Carers (Equal Opportunities) Act 2004 and its potential to empower carers in combining caring with wider life opportunities.

www.mssociety.org.uk
www.carersuk.org
www.crossroads.org.uk
www.carers.org
www.rethink.org
www.macmillan.org.uk
www.helptheaged.org.uk

Portsmouth Healthcare Trust and Portsmouth's **Alzheimer's Society** have signed a partnership agreement to work in tandem in providing an occupational therapist (OT) and support worker to work with users and carers to enhance a joined-up care plan for dementia sufferers. The project has carers on the joint care team and has arranged open evenings to provide a window on the project. Carers have a clear role in feeding back their views of service efficacy.

www.portshosp.org.uk
www.alzheimers.org.uk

The **'Supporting Carers Better' Network** is a mental health project that consists of an information exchange and contacting service that provides information and training for those who work with carers (voluntary and paid) and puts otherwise isolated carers in touch with wider networks. The project also facilitates a range of carer skills and training in good practice. The service is supported by Together: Working for well-being.

www.together-uk.org
www.scbnetwork.org/about/index.cfm

Swansea Council for Voluntary Service (SCVS) has formed an umbrella group called the Mental Health Forum and Development Services to respond to the challenges set out in the NSF for mental health. It covers the Neath and Swansea areas and has carer participation and the development of participation as two of its principal goals. SCVS itself is promoting interagency collaboration involving both statutory and voluntary sectors.

www.scvs.org.uk/representpart/p1540/mhf.html

In recognition of the age profile of the locality (the highest proportion of older people in the West Midlands) and the likely weight of carer input, and also responding to the large BME population in the West Midlands, the **Princess Royal Trust Sandwell Carers' Centre** has appointed a care development worker specifically to work with older carers. It works closely with the elderly persons' coordinator located in a GP surgery.

www.carers.org/sandwell

The **Kingston User and Carer Forum** supports and involves carers who are working with a family member or friend with a mental health problem. The forum is made up of users and carers in Kingston upon Thames and aims to mentor those new to the role or facing challenges while caring for a person with a mental health problem. The forum works closely with South West London and St George's Mental Health Trust in furthering user and carer involvement in service planning and delivery.

www.kingston.gov.uk/scope.doc

Basildon Princess Royal Trust and Castle Point Carers' Centre responded to the need to involve GPs in identifying and referring more carers in their daily work. They made contact with all local practice managers and, with some intensive work with GPs and health centres, raised the profile of carer needs by getting leaflets, information packs and posters sited in surgeries. This resulted in a number of previously unknown carers making their first contact with the carers' centre.

www.carers.org

Gateshead NHS Trust/Gateshead Social Services discharge liaison nurses work with voluntary-sector organisations – for example, Age Concern and the local carers' association – to aid smooth discharges and ensure more carer-friendly discharge plans. Carers are consulted on the efficacy of discharge planning, and their views on how best to improve discharge planning further are canvassed. In addition, Gateshead Social Services work with the NHS to collate data on the number of carer assessments completed by hospital social workers.

www.gatesheadhealth.nhs.uk

North and West Belfast Health and Social Services Trust's consultation report *Supporting carers* responds to carers' expressed concern that they require more training in both health and social care interventions. The trust is committed to working with them to explore current and future training needs to minimise the more negative aspects of caring.

www.nwb.n-i.nhs.uk/carers/supportingcarershomepage.html

The **Alzheimer's Society** nationally established a helpline for all those caring for people with dementia (old *and* young). Alzheimer's Nottinghamshire has begun the process of establishing a local carers' telephone network to help embed mutual carer support in a localised way. An extended carer telephone network is seen as enhancing the participation of dementia carers who, due to paid work commitments, may be unlikely to access local Alzheimer's daytime facilities.

www.alzheimers.org.uk

The **Bradford Health Action Zone** (HAZ; Bradford NHS Trust) project, which helps family carers from minority ethnic groups, has established BME support groups to offer culturally sensitive support and learning materials to aid carers working with people with dementia. The project canvasses the views of carers while making them aware of key information on service developments. Family carers receive support and are themselves encouraged to snowball support through support group involvement.

www.haznet.org.uk/hazs/hazmap/h_brad.asp

Alzheimer's Sheffield and the **Northern General Hospital** (Sheffield) aim to take intermediate care into the community to enhance dementia services. Parallel work with a local dementia resource centre aims to provide carers and dementia professionals with a forum to share their views and influence professional working.

www.alzheimers.org.uk

Alzheimer's Huddersfield provides respite care for carers that gives them the opportunity to reflect on the caring role through reminiscence work with other carers. The project has boosted the self-esteem and voice of carers in the wider caring context.

www.alzheimers.org.uk

4.2 Consultation with feedback or exploration of outcomes

In addition to their carer forums, generous expense repayment scheme and 'Carers as trainers' programme, the **Norfolk Health Trust**, **Norfolk County Council** and **Norfolk Carers Partnership** are planning to take carer participation a step further by focusing on the outcomes of carer involvement. This way, provision and carer experiences of participation should be more easily quantified and go beyond paying lip service to carers' needs.

www.norfolk.gov.uk

Torbay Interagency Carers Strategy identified carer support workers (CSWs) as having a key policy and practice role in both identifying and supporting carers. With initial funding from Torbay Social Services and a bidding process that encouraged interested GPs to take on CSWs, they helped establish 15 CSWs in 2002/03. An evaluation of carer impact established that carers in contact with CSWs (compared to those not in contact) had reduced levels of stress, and wider health problems were also lessened. The success of the initiative has led to a long-term compact between Torbay PCT and SSD in the joint funding of further CSW posts.

www.torbay.gov.uk
www.idea-knowledge.gov.uk/idk/aio/1704923

Alongside established carer newsletters, information booklets and carer membership on local implementation teams (LITs), **Carers in Hertfordshire** and the **Stevenage Primary Care Trust** have founded the 'Nothing Registered – Nothing Gained' campaign, which aims to maximise carers' awareness of the benefits of primary care recognition of their carer status. Carers in Hertfordshire has also hosted carer awareness training with local nursing staff who work closely with carers. In addition, parent carer work has helped enhance carers' voice in transition planning with Hertfordshire County Council.

http://www.carersinherts.org.uk/

Somerset County Council social services/carers consultation survey produced detailed carer profiles with which to plan and respond to future care needs. The research survey provides a depth of insights into not simply what care needs are or are not assessed, offered and reviewed, but why carers felt they were unable to access the support and involvement that they felt they deserved. Most important was a commitment on behalf of Somerset County Council social services to involve carers in reviewing and improving services in light of the problems highlighted in the survey.

www.somerset.gov.uk

As part of its 'Partners in care' campaign with the Princess Royal Trust, the **Royal College of Psychiatrists** has committed to developing a code of conduct for professionals working with carers on the sorts of issues and solutions carers might reasonably raise in their caring role for someone with a mental health problem. Carers will also be involved in the basic training of psychiatrists to raise awareness of and appropriate professional responses to carer issues.

http://www.rcpsych.ac.uk/campaigns/partnersincare.aspx

Sunderland City Hospitals NHS Trust have appointed a senior (director-level) member of staff as a carer lead. Alongside this symbolic commitment is ongoing consultation with Sunderland carers to establish future carer needs. The trust works closely with **Sunderland City Council** (recently awarded Beacon status for its carer support) and the **Sunderland Carers' Centre** to further joined-up working (for example single assessment group) around carers' issues and focuses on the outcomes of involving carers. The city council is fully committed to engaging carers in a broader and deeper partnership in the future.

www.sunderland.nhs.uk/carers/publications/carers_week_conference_report.pdf
www.sunderland.gov.uk/Pages/press/pritem.asp?id=706

South West Yorkshire Mental Health NHS Trust commissioned research into the impact of carer and user involvement in trust research. The study highlighted the advantages of carer involvement to date, but noted that it largely takes the form of consultation rather than playing a formative role in research that informs early service planning and development. The study (2003) is being used to embed carer and user involvement in research and to emphasise the direct impact of involvement on the research process and service and involvement more generally.

www.southwestyorkshire.nhs.uk

4.3 Participation

Worcestershire County Council has worked with carers and user groups to formulate a 'kitemark' accreditation standard for carer/user involvement. The standard has been squarely based on carer/user ideas about key elements of

successful involvement and will be awarded and reviewed by these groups.
The standard is being flagged as helpful in identifying those organisations in
Worcestershire who are involved in successful activity.

www.worcestershire.gov.uk

Milton Keynes City Council's carer-led research review of short breaks provides a
very tangible example of carers being centrally involved in the framing, completion
and recommendations outlined in a research report. This is a good example of health
and social care professionals and carers working together in partnership. The research
was careful to include the views and voices of ordinarily 'hard-to-reach' carers – for
example, those in the BME community. Producing less tangible, but perhaps just
as important, results, the 'Carers' Journey' event run by the **Milton Keynes Carers
Action Group** (consisting of representatives from the city council, the Milton Keynes
Primary Care Trust, Crossroads, Age Concern, etc) provided an opportunity for
carers to reflect on their lives as carers and to look at gaps in service provision. To
encourage attendance alternative therapies were included as an integral part of the
event.

www.mkcarers.org

East Glamorgan Mental Health Directorate (Rhondda Cynon) has committed to
involving carers of people with dementia in the interviewing and recruitment of
new nursing appointments. Full training and educational support are provided to
interested carers.

www.rhondda-cynon-taff.gov.uk/stellent/groups/Public/documents/hcst/split_
content_en.hcst?pid=CSP0&sid=&tid=

Hackney Borough Council aims to respond to concerns that user and carer
involvement only takes place once service ideas and plans were in place. As a result,
it has formed user and carer groups to work with staff in visiting existing services and
planning future service developments at the outset.

www.hackney.gov.uk

The **Suffolk Family Carers Mental Health Project** provides a countywide service
for carers, giving them access to one-to-one and group support, advocacy and
information. It facilitates training for a range of users and carers to provide skills and
confidence in working with mental health professionals in both the statutory and
voluntary sectors.

www.suffolk-carers.co.uk/suffolkcarers/mentalhealth/mhteam.htm

Rochdale Borough Council has made a commitment to expand the use of service
quality networks and to involve fully users and carers in setting, evaluating and
monitoring service standards for carers in the borough. It has also committed to a
fuller involvement of people with learning difficulties in the selection, recruitment
and training of staff in all agencies.

www.rochdale.gov.uk/docs/living/bchsfnl.doc

A newly appointed specialist carer support officer for **Harrogate Carers Resource**
(Princess Royal Trust) was recruited, managed, trained and supported by the carers

of the centre. Firm cooperation and partnership working with local primary health professionals is a key facet of this work and has spread to other geographical areas due to the success of the role.

www.carers.org

The **Alzheimer's Society Lesbian and Gay Carers' Network** has established a telephone befriending service and a dedicated web page for gay/lesbian carers, and network members are funded to carry out speaking engagements to share experiences and raise awareness of lesbian and gay carers' needs. **Body Positive Cheshire & North Wales (Crewe)** provides support, advice, information and advocacy for carers of people with HIV/AIDS.

gaycarers@alzheimers.org.uk (email)
www.bpcnw.co.uk

5 Carer participation: Practice survey

5.1 Introduction

The following is a practice survey of current carer participation in England, Wales and Northern Ireland. The survey relates evidence of carer participation from both the statutory and the voluntary sectors and provides examples of best practice and also evidence of factors that continue to limit carer participation. Adopting a framework for analysing carer participation informed by the work of Arnstein (152), Goss and Miller (81), Casey (153) and the Audit Commission (154), this survey (and the wider position paper) was intended to set a standard for involving and including carers.

The carers in the CPRG decided at their first meeting that they wanted to be primarily involved in the practice survey so that they could relate findings to their own experiences. The need for this involvement was illustrated at a very early stage. A questionnaire was initially drawn up by the research team and presented to the CPRG for discussion. Participants made clear that the original questions would not result in the information sought, as illustrated by the following:

> The research team came to us with the start of a questionnaire. We said, 'No, if you ask the questions in those ways, you won't get answers that mean anything'.
>
> Carer A, CPRG

From this point, the research and the practice survey became the carers' review, supported by the academic research team, as the following comments testify:

> We all felt that the questions came from the carers and were therefore appropriate ... we were working as a team and all knew that the work we were doing had significance ... carers provide a different perspective ... which can lead to a deeper understanding.
>
> Carer D, CPRG

> I would like to say, at all stages in the research, the research team have listened to us carers and not tried to force their views and opinions on us. So thank you for allowing me to take part and I hope my taking part has been of some help.
>
> Carer C, CPRG

5.2 Summary of survey methodology and methods

The methodology has been summarised in the introduction to this Position Paper, and a full account of the methodology and methods used is given in Appendix G.

Questionnaires were sent to all SSDs in England and Wales, and to a selection* of the following:

- PCTs and health trusts in England and Wales
- joint care trusts in England and Wales

* A selection had to be made as there are many hundreds of PCTs, JCTs, health boards, LDPBs, etc. See the section on response rates below for all selection criteria.

- health boards in Northern Ireland
- LDPBs
- voluntary organisations
- carers' organisations.

5.2.1 Response rates

Table 1
Response rates

Organisation	Number (Qs) despatched	Number returned (valid)	Percentage (valid)
SSD	164	67	41%
PCT and health authority/trust*	108	32	30%
Health and social care trust/ board and/or JCT*	17	10	60%
LDPB	37	9	25%
Voluntary organisation	35	2	5%
Carers' organisation	105	16	15%

Note: *Data categories have been aggregated for overview purposes.

Despite several attempts to follow up voluntary organisations (excluding carers' organisations), the response rate remained poor and it is difficult to speculate why. One of those that did respond worked only with young carers so would have been excluded anyway. Interestingly the one organisation that returned a valid response worked with gay and lesbian users and put the researchers in touch with the worker for the Alzheimer's Society Gay and Lesbian Network.

A geographical breakdown of respondent statutory organisations is given in Appendix I.

Following the return of the questionnaire (n=138), members of the research team conducted 63 telephone interviews with statutory organisations' (n=35) carers' centres (n=10). These interviews included 18 interviews with carers. As these interviewees were the only group researched who were directly engaged in caring, it was felt that interview matching and sensitivity would be enhanced by using carers as interviewers. Indeed members of the CPRG led this initiative to involve carers in these interview contexts. The latter were trained in interview techniques, and agreed research protocols were adhered to. An iterative interview checking process was put in place to ensure inter-interview comparability and standards were maintained.

5.3 Introducing findings

The findings from the questionnaire and telephone interviews have been pulled together under the following headings:

- Defining carers
- Carer participation and infrastructure
- Embedding carer issues
- Support for carers in involvement and participation
- Reaching 'hidden' or marginalised carers
- Agreeing outcomes and providing feedback
- Accountability
- Carers' assessments
- Financial constraints
- Training of staff in carer participation and involvement
- Emergency planning
- Sharing and developing good practice

5.3.1 Defining 'carers'

The need to look at how organisations defined 'carers' was established early on by the CPRG because of some personal experiences of carers in the group, who saw themselves as marginalised. In addition, when the fullest range of carer contexts was explored, it was discovered that the definition of carer needed to encapsulate the home, healthcare and day care environments where carers may find themselves. The primacy of carer influence in arriving at carer definitions is shown in the following:

> The research team have listened to us, the carers, and not tried to enforce their views or opinions on us. If we wanted something changed we thought was not right, it was changed without question. The definition of 'carer' is one thing that springs to mind. We spent a great deal of time on this one point alone. In the end, it was the carers' point that won the day.
>
> Carer B, CPRG

The results suggest that, of the valid responses, all but one SSD have a written definition. This is reassuring given the requirements of the legislation and guidance under which SSDs operate. Written definitions were also in use in a majority of NHS trusts and JCTs. Perhaps surprisingly, PCTs claimed not to be operating with written definitions of carers. The one health board respondent from Northern Ireland was not currently using a written definition of a carer. (Percentages for this respondent category should, of course, be treated with caution given the low number of respondents)

There was some diversity in the definitions of 'carers', but the most commonly cited were those from statutory or major voluntary sector sources. There seems to be four different types of definition in use. The first, in widespread use, emphasises both the unpaid nature of caring and the need for support because of a carer's circumstances:

Table 2
Does your organisation have a written definition of the word 'carer'?
(Total eligible population in brackets. Note: Not all respondents
answered)

Type of organisation	Number (responding to question)	Percentage
SSD	66 (67)	98.5%
NHS health authority/trust	9 (16)	56.3%
PCT	0 (16)	0%
Health and social care trust/ board and/or JCT	8 (10)	80%
LDPB	5 (9)	55.5%
Carers' organisation	15 (16)	94%

> A carer is someone who, without payment, provides help and support to a friend,
> neighbour or relative who could not manage otherwise because of frailty, illness or
> disability.
>
> Princess Royal Trust

The second definition relates to key statutory thresholds of 'substantial' user
and carer needs. The term 'substantial' also features widely in related legislation
(Chronically Sick and Disabled Persons Act, 1970):

> A carer is a person who provides or intends to provide a substantial amount of care
> to another person on a regular basis, other than as an employee or under contract
> or as a voluntary organisation.
>
> Carers (Recognition and Services) Act 1995

Similar definitions also made reference to the minimum age of the carer, to help
distinguish younger from adult carers (18 years or over). References to the care needs
of children (service users) was also mentioned by reference to section 17 (11) of the
Children Act 1989 and the Carers and Disabled Children Act 2000. Parent carers
were explicitly mentioned by one SSD (SSD 55, London borough) under the question
on defining carers. Other authorities specifically talk about the needs of disabled
children and the substantial caring implications that often stem from childhood
disability (SSD 49, South East).

The question of interpreting 'substantial' and 'regular' care was an interesting and
challenging one. The absence of detailed definitions of these terms was used by some
departments to foster flexibility in the interpretation of care needs – for example:

> The council has recognised that every caring situation is different and the impact
> of caring will vary from individual to individual. It is a matter of professional
> practice to identify the impact of the caring role in light of the carer's age, general
> health, employment status, interests and other responsibilities and commitments.
>
> SSD 11, South Central England

In [council name], the LA works to a loose definition that relies on carers' views as to whether or not they are carers.

SSD 63, North West England

The carers literature makes clear the lack of an agreed working definition of carers and professional differences in the way carers are perceived. As Twigg and Atkin (75) make clear, professionals may view carers as resources, co-workers or co-clients, all of which suggests differing levels of likely engagement with carers and their role in decision making.

Perhaps more unexpected were definitions that very occasionally strayed from the official starting point:

A carer is someone of any age who provides a great deal of care for a close family member, relative or friend on a regular basis without payment.

SSD 59, North West England

The third type of definition emphasises both the diversity of carers and the responsibility they take on in caring for others:

A carer is someone of any age who takes responsibility for looking after a person who cannot manage in their daily living without help because of an illness, disability, special need or frailty.

Carers' centre definition

Finally, a fourth definition was identified that focused on the diverse and universal nature of caring. The definition also highlights the needs of carers and the impact of caring on the extent of their social inclusion:

Carers are found in all communities. Invariably their lives are restricted. Many people who care do not identify as carers.

Carers UK

The question of diversity was also evident in definitions that emphasised the range of users who commonly require unpaid care:

A carer may be a relative, friend or neighbour who provides substantial care for someone with physical disabilities, learning disabilities, mental health problems or [is] an older person.

SSD 15, South West England

People who look after a friend, relative, child or partner who is ill, frail, has a disability or misuses drugs or alcohol.

SSD 64, London borough

Overall, then, there is no one agreed definition of carer. Indeed, the commentary from the CPRG suggested that one's definition rather depended on the standpoint one had and one's proximity to sources of professional power. Clearly professionals continue to shroud definitional thresholds of 'substantial' and 'regular' in some secrecy.

Definitions varied, often reflecting the diverse settings within England, Wales and Northern Ireland and the very disparate populations that may occur even in a given geographical region. Of note were some unique responses that emanated from Northern Ireland, in which definitions of the term 'carer' included those traumatised by the 'troubles' among those who are cared for (JCT 7, Northern Ireland).

Since the responses were comprehensive in the questionnaire findings, the question was not investigated further in the telephone interviews.

5.3.2 Carer participation and infrastructure

Organisations were asked if they encouraged and supported carer participation. All respondent organisations laid claim to this (although the extent of participation varied). The scope for self-selection of organisations suggests some caution is required, however. It cannot be assumed that non-respondents were similarly engaged in participation. Furthermore, carers' organisations had a rather different perception about the level and extent to which their partners operated participation. For example, while 13 out of 16 (83%) agreed that SSDs involved carers in 'stages of service planning and delivery', only 4 (25%) suggested that health organisations were doing so (*see* Appendix H).

> We had a young carers project funded by the PCT but they withdrew the funding. We felt they didn't see carers as that central to their brief....
>
> Carers' centre 10, North East England

To gain insights into the nature of carer participation, we asked a range of questions about infrastructure, which begin to illuminate the extent of activity. First, 'How long have you involved/included carers?':

Table 3 shows that carers' organisations and SSDs are most likely to have had participation in place for more than five years. Of SSDs, 98.5% had been undertaking such activity for more than one year. Health organisations, PCTs and NHS trusts were either slightly less likely to have been operating for more than five years or much less likely in the case of JCTs and the one health board respondent. The gap narrows for PCTs and SSDs, however, if we compare those who have been involved in carer participation for more than one year. Even JCTs and the one health board respondent had mostly been engaged in carer participation for at least one year. These figures reflect the literature, which points to the growing quantity of carer participation activity (references 51, 75, 195, 199). This coverage should not, however, be read as evidence of a depth of carer involvement.

We then went on to look at whether the commitment to including and involving carers was written into official documents, and whether these were stand-alone documents (for example, a carers' strategy, where a commitment has to be shown) or in a range of policies and procedures, which might suggest a commitment beyond the minimum requirement. The majority of respondents (>95%) said that their commitments were written into more than one document. An example of these documents is provided in Appendix J.

Table 3
How long have you involved/included carers?

Type of organisation	More than 5 years	Between 1 and 5 years	Less than 1 year	Total
SSD	28 (41.8%)	38 (56.7%)	1 (1.5%)	67 (67)
PCT	4 (33.3%)	8 (66.7%)	0 (0.0%)	12 (16)
NHS trust	5 (31.3%)	9 (56.3%)	2 (12.5%)	16 (16)
JCT	2 (22.2%)	6 (66.7%)	1 (11.1%)	9
Health and social care board/ trust	0 (0.0%)	1 (100%)	0 (0.0%)	1
Carers' organisation	15 (94%)	1 (6%)	0	16

Note:
LDPBs were not asked this question because their inception was after the issuing of *Valuing people* (2001).

Regional differences were evident. The North West, London and Eastern England had all been operating with carer involvement for more than one year. In contrast, in the Midlands,15.4% have been operating for less than one year. The region operating carer participation longest – over five years – was the North East of England.

While most of the respondent organisations pointed to high levels of recording of commitments to carer participation, it is noteworthy that response rates were very low for PCTs (16%). Telephone interviews helped explain this to some extent: most PCTs tended to defer to and draw on SSD documentation. An example of this is given in Appendix J.

Another useful benchmark of the level of carer participation might be gauged by the extent to which carers have direct access to key decision-making forums. An example of this is given in Appendix K.

Table 4
If you do involve carers, or intend to, are your commitments written into your official documents? (Percentages in brackets. NB: The asterisk indicates non-responses)

Organisation	Yes	No	Total
SSD	62 (96.9%)	2 (3.1%)	64* (67)
PCT	1 (50%)	1 (50%)	2* (16)
NHS trust	11 (100%)	0	11* (16)
JCT	7 (78%)	2 (22%)	7* (9)
Health boards	1	0	1 (1)
LDPB	9 (100%)	0	9 (9)
Carers' organisation	16 (100%)	0	16 (16)

Table 5
Do carers have a direct form of access to key decision-making forums?
(Percentages and overall totals are in brackets. Carers' organisations were
not asked this question directly, as their members make up the bodies
seeking representation)

Organisation	Direct access: Yes	Direct access: No	Total
SSD	61 (93.8%)	4 (6.2%)	65 (67)
PCT	11 (91.7%)	1 (8.3%)	12 (16)
Health board	1 (100%)	0 (0.0%)	1 (1)
NHS trust	14 (93.3%)	1 (6.7%)	15 (16)
JCT	7 (87.5%)	1 (12.5%)	8 (9)
LDPB	9 (100%)	0	9 (9)

The vast majority of LAs have carer strategy groups or forums in place, although
the degree of activity and effectiveness of these varied enormously. These bodies
take an overview of carers' issues and may or may not also have responsibility for
ensuring that carers are part of more specific policy-making groupings – for example,
impairment- or task-specific groupings. Most (>90%) talked about involving carers in
a number of forums, many of which are service area-specific –for example, mental
health. Below are examples of both types. Examples of a range of forums can be
found in Appendix K.

> The local carers' centre [name] runs a carers advisory forum every two months
> which is open to carers to come and give their views.... The views are fed into the
> statutory service planning processes. The process works both ways in that views
> may come up spontaneously and will get fed in, or the statutory services may
> decide to consult carers on specific issues and will approach the carers advisory
> forum for carers' views.
>
> SSD 11, English Midlands

It is noteworthy that the above SSD adopts an *ad hoc* approach to involving carers
once a decision has been made on what to involve carers in. Arguably, to achieve
higher forms of partnership (*see* Arnstein's 'citizen power' stage, reference 152),
carers might also be asked what they might reasonably be expected to be consulted
on. That is, agenda setting can more fully involve carers in deciding what are pivotal
issues for involvement. It is also important that carer input includes both strategic
and street-level participation:

> We have a number of forums in which carers can have both strategic and day-
> to-day input into care planning and practice: the NSF users/carers group, the EMI
> elderly mentally infirm carers subgroup, the LD (learning disability) partnership
> board, Partnership and Positive Ageing group, mental health carers liaison group.
>
> SSD 35, North West England

On paper, therefore, there does seem to be access to both strategic and street-level forums in some localities. Some 94% of SSDs stated that carers had access to key decision-making forums, and over 90% of the various health authorities, JCTs and PCTs stated this (see Table 3 above). Access to street-level forums such as carer centre forums was mentioned less often, but it may be that organisations were responding strategically. What the percentage does not show was how easy it was for carers to make use of those forums, either through their own endeavours or through the participation of other carers on their behalf.

5.3.3 Embedding carer issues

An often-repeated message that came from carers, carers' organisations and some social and health professionals was that paper commitments were often not translated into substantive changes. This is reflected in the literature (51, 155, 178, 179, 184, 199, 202), which makes clear how common a gap between the rhetoric and the reality of involvement really is. Thus while the above provides some insights into the range of participation, the researchers wanted to try and explore commitment in more depth and discover how it manifested itself.

Some SSDs (n=5) mentioned the employment of workers (sometimes called 'carer involvement officers' or 'carer coordination officers') specifically to embed carer involvement into everyday practice. It is worth noting that PCTs tended to fund more carers' support workers (n=9) that other bodies did, but this may be because more LAs are devolving monies to carers' organisations to employ workers. It is an issue that requires further study.

One defining factor of commitment might be how well carers' issues are embedded into partnership arrangements between agencies. Telephone interviews explored this issue further and an example of good partnership working is provided here:

Partnership working

A large social and health care directorate with a largely urban catchment area has a well-established partnership approach to user and carer participation, with the involvement of carers going back to the late 1980s, anticipating the NHS and Community Care Act 1990. The development of a special project on community care was supported by the LA, but also had the backing of key members of the UK disabled people's movement. Other key drivers were the National Carers Strategy and the Carers (Recognition and Services) Act 1995.

The directorate has developed excellent links with the local PCTs, with the latter providing significant funds for carer development work alongside SSD funding. This funding has remained constant since the inception of the PCTs, which now provide three carer support workers covering the entire area.

The staff responsible for 'service user and carer involvement' established a thriving carers' centre run by a consortium of voluntary sector organisations. A carers' association brings together these voices, and is underpinned by advocacy principles.

The centre receives a Carers Grant and PCT and additional *ad hoc* external funding. There is a service-level agreement between the SSD and the carers' centre.

The centre is a successful one-stop shop for carers, providing information, advice, respite funding guidance/contacts, links with wider health and social care agencies and carer input into both strategic and street-level decision-making forums. The social care and health directorate builds carer comments into future carer documentation and policy wherever possible and practicable. Wider business improvement models are translated into specific improvements to carer participation programmes, outcomes and impact.

SSD 17, English Midlands

A similar picture was provided by 35 SSDs where partnership arrangements are in place between certain groups, as the following examples make clear:

We work closely with health, voluntary and wider social services, we have responded well to carers and we included a section in our carers strategy on recognition. Age Concern suggested a section on working carers, which was included, and the strategy was very much customised to the requests of the various contributors.... We target hidden carers and are looking to appoint a carers outreach worker. The council has a tendering process for domiciliary care, and they consulted with carers and carers organisations and these [contributions] were included in the decision-making process....

SSD 59, North West England

and ... [We have] ... used Health Act flexibilities to develop a structure of pooled budgets and service user boards. These boards are responsible for the strategic direction of health and social care.... The partnership has supported carers' engagement within all of these processes ... in all aspects of strategic development, service development and quality assurance.

SSD 8, English Pennines

This second example above reflects some of the examples of best practice in the literature, which highlight the challenges and successes of partnership working, both interprofessionally and between client and professional (167, 214). Partnership working that displays a significant amount of carer influence is also evident in the next two examples. The first, in particular, illustrates the creative partnership established in commissioning services:

Carers are encouraged to be involved in all areas of service planning and the commissioning of services from external providers. During the recent tendering process with external providers, carers were involved in formulating the service specifications, interview questions and with the interview process.... We have developed our 'How was it for you?' guidelines for effective working with users and carers.

SSD 15, South West England

When we meet with partner agencies through the carer strategy group, we ensure the full involvement of health, the voluntary sector and social services. In response to carers, we included a section in the strategy on recognition, with values and objectives very much a product of carers' views.

JCT 4, North West England

The following quote details how the principles of involvement have been translated into practice and assessment flexibilities. The issue of responsive assessment was made clear in the carers literature (67, 173, 174, 179, 226):

We are a relatively new authority and have always been big on involvement and responsive to local needs.... We began with tenants' involvement, but imported that principle into user and carer involvement in the mid-1990s.... We work in partnership by being flexible about the definition of carer, especially where carers are under obvious stress. We work closely with mental health workers and OTs and use the Carers Grant in part to fund training for these important workers.

SSD 11, English Midlands

... and in the perspectives on good partnership working of carers' organisations:

We have a fruitful relationship with both social services and our PCTs and have director-level sign-up to working with carers. We have a carers' champion who sits on all major meetings, PCT, acute trusts and learning disability partnership board. We commissioned a carers survey, and although we only got a 23% response rate, 77% of carers reported that social services department's work with them was 'helpful or better'....

Carers' centre staff 1/carer 1

Other positive partnership comments related to more specific and focused activity:

One example of collaboration is that of our work with [name of PCT] on the 'Health Promotion Programmes for Carers' by Healthy [name of PCT] Service and, by the spring [of] 2003, through the development of 'Home as a Workplace' training, which is recorded in the joint carers strategy.

SSD 62, London borough

A few organisations mentioned partnership working through the modernisation and reform group (MARG) structure, as the following example notes:

Embedding carer issues

This medium-sized LA in North East England has a largely urban population, a high prevalence of disability and very high deprivation indicators in a number of its localities. It has very good working relationship with the local carers' centre to which it provides core funding.

The LA has followed the modernisation agendas in health and social care by introducing 16 modernisation and reform groups, or MARGs. These focus on diverse user groups – for example, older people and disabled people – and the development of services to these groups.

Part of the MARG philosophy and practice is to ensure that carers' issues and voices are fed through to adjacent MARGs.

The crossover links built into the their activities ensure that carer priorities, concerns and service needs are referred to and acted on by other MARGs within the authority. The LA has no specific carers strategy as this is seen as reinforcing the attachment of carers' issues to only one or two key forums. As the LA respondent noted: "Each service group *must* show how it is going to measure carer involvement and must have carers on their membership".

Corroborative evidence supports the view expressed by the LA that carers' views are facilitated and responded to in both health and social care agencies. In addition, the *People first* agenda has also provided wider LA support for carers from leisure services and education departments – for example, free access for carers to their facilities.

SSD 61, North East England

And on joint working expressed by a health trust:

Prior to 2002, funding for carers work was patchy – soft money that came from a number of sources and through a bidding process. Post-2002, there has been a 'watershed' with the development of the TPCT [teaching primary care trust]. We work closely with [name] social services around carers' support and involvement. We are looking at joint funding from SSD and TPCT grants. We have MARGs which emphasise multiagency working. Our patient/carer involvement team has seven staff ... we are building joint teams to respond to both health and social needs.

TPCT 11, North East England

This authority working closely with the local carers' organisation subsequently went on to receive Beacon status for its work with carers, with the following quote taken from the Beacon status feedback:

> The use of modernisation and reform groups to redesign service provision using a multi–agency approach shows how the council excels in strategic planning and involving carers in that process.
>
> Feedback on Beacon council application, SSD 61, North East England

Although MARGs no doubt operate in other LAs they were, unlike the above, very rarely mentioned in the context of carer participation (*n*=5). It is noteworthy that there is also scant mention of MARG structures in the carer literature. This may, however, be a question of the terminology that LAs use.

The following example shows the use of a similar cross-cutting structure as a way to begin to redress the previously 'difficult' process of carer involvement. In response to some 'staff resistance to involvement', this JCT has embedded carer issues as follows:

> As carers' coordinator I work across five strands of the [name of organisation]'s work – that includes physical disability, learning disability, elderly, family and childcare and mental health. Although it is early days, by positioning my development role into all five care strands, this gives the trust more scope to raise the profile of carers.
>
> JCT 7, Northern Ireland

Interestingly seven organisations mentioned difficulties in partnership working with other agencies. These were the ones that were having the most struggles in achieving carers' participation and involvement, as the example below shows:

> Health [PCTs] have a different view to SSDs. They are very client-focused but emphasise confidentiality. This does create problems as we pride ourselves on talking to others and working holistically.
>
> SSD 11, English Midlands

> The PCT does part-fund the [name] carers' centre. However, we have been disappointed that they decided to pull their funding for one element of the centre's activity. We have the perception that there is some lack of interest and that carers are not seen as PCT 'core business'.
>
> SSD 41, North East England

What cannot be determined is whether non-respondents were similarly engaged in such high levels of partnership working or, indeed, in very low levels. This may be an area for further exploration.

Unsurprisingly, very strong partnerships were mentioned by six out of nine PBs where a mandate for partnership working is clearly central to the process:

Partnership working

This large NHS partnership trust with a particular brief in providing mental health services has strong links with carers and other statutory service providers. Alongside an awareness of the details of statutory guidance on definitions of care and partnership, the trust prides itself on 'caring about caring'. The definition of 'carer' and decisions on the interpretation of both legislation and guidance are handled by the CPA steering group, which has carer representation.

A carer adviser sits on the main trust board in addition to membership of the carers advisory group. Carer issues are embedded In most key documents, not simply specific ones. Implementation groups ensure that strategies are put into practice and monitored. The carers advisory group is co-chaired by representatives of the county council and the hospital trust. In making key board appointments, particular attention is given to equal opportunities and avoiding under-representation by gender, ethnicity and disability status.

Close and successful working between trust and county council were behind the joint formulation of both the carers advisory group and the content of the CPA documents. 'Concerns raised about lack of clarity for the public and staff about respective responsibilities of the network of providers concerned with 'having a voice' [that is, Patient Advisory Liaison Service [PALS], complaints, ICAS, Advocacy] led to a multi-agency meeting and commitment to producing a simple information leaflet (*verbatim*).

Joint working in enhancing vocational services received positive accolades from the Office of the Deputy Prime Minister, and reflected joint working in response to the Green Paper on employment and disabled people. Collaborative working has also improved day services so that carers now have greater flexibility and choices.

NHS partnership trust 16, Eastern England

In other PBs, carer issues are embedded via a diverse range of activities.

Carers have a direct say in the key decision making on the partnership board. The chair of the carers' group is a carer, and sits on the project implementation board. There are five carer seats on the partnership board. We have a carers' conference each year, and we have a carers' network to give and receive information. I am the vice chair of the board and also a carer....

PB 2, English Midlands

Certain groups were mentioned more often as being at the leading edge of carer participation/involvement. Most commonly cited were carers of people with learning difficulties, which is explicable in part by the specific service standards contained in the *Valuing people* White Paper (2001), and carers of people with mental health problems, due in part to the specific standard in the NSF for mental health (1999).

However, most of the substantial literature on mental health and carers omits this point (68, 146, 155, 163, 171, 172, 191, 192, 205, 233, 243, 248):

> In mental health in [name of authority] there is a history of involvement. Carers were keen to get involved and do things. We wanted to let carers take the lead....
>
> JCT 8, North East England

> In learning difficulties, we have to feedback to other carers in the carers' forum ... we are very far ahead in learning difficulties, the same in mental health where there is a standard specifically about carers.
>
> SSD 53, English Midlands

> Carers are consulted with regard to the Carers Grant – in particular, people with learning difficulties – discussing what sort of support carers require.
>
> SSD 58, London borough

Driven by *Valuing people* (2001), learning disability PBs responses tended to reflect both the principles and practice that applies to carer participation and partnership in general. One issue that was frequently raised by social services respondents is that of successfully widening out the activity of the PBs to take account of the broader constituencies of carers and users. Below is the kind of comment typical of the SSD and PB respondents interviewed:

> We have a history in [name of learning disability services] of working with family carers. We discuss what we are doing with carers and other statutory agencies. However, there is feeling here that older people's services may be left behind because of the push on learning difficulties and mental health. We are struggling to get older people's services on board.
>
> PB 2, English Midlands

The challenge then is one of continuing to respond to key policy guidance – for example, *Valuing people* and the NSF for mental health (1999) – but also to ensure that the commitment to carers is more than rhetorical in LAs' responses to user groups who may not be caring for a targeted client group. For instance, one respondent – PB 8, English Pennines – answered 'Yes' to most questions about carer participation and has carers represented at all levels of service planning, but makes little reference to carers and their needs in their main document on learning disability services.

5.3.4 Support for carers in involvement and participation

One key factor in encouraging carers to become involved in decision-making forums is the scope for carers to buy in replacement care to cover their time commitments. Respondents were asked whether they made resources available for carers to be actively involved.

Table 6
Do you make resources available for carers to be actively involved?
(Percentages and total eligible populations in brackets)

Organisation	Yes	No	Total
SSD	63 (95.5%)	3 (4.5%)	66 (67)
PCT	10 (90.9%)	1 (9.1%)	11 (16)
NHS trust	13 (81.3%)	3 (18.8%)	16 (16)
JCT	7 (100%)	0 (.0%)	7 (9)
Health board	1 (100%)	0 (0%)	1 (1)
LDPB	9 (100%)	0 (0%)	9 (9)
Carers' organisation	16 (100%)	0 (0%)	16 (16)

Funding individual carer's time was the prevalent form of resource support. This was paid either directly or through carers' organisations. Carers Grant monies were the main source of revenue. There has been little discrete academic attention paid to the question of expenses payments (146). The following was typical of responses from LAs:

> Resources made available to carers to enable them to participate include: travel expenses, a sitting service – increasingly through direct payments. The council have introduced a 'looser' audit trail to enable funds to be used more flexibly and on an individual basis.
>
> SSD 11, South East England

However, the difficulties faced by carers in becoming involved should not be underestimated. Below are typical comments:

> The council run a users' and carers' forum. The organisation uses this to inform decision making across the council.... [We] have representatives from different carer organisations on different groups, who take issues back to their organisations and give feedback, which is then returned in the feedback loop ... but we are finding it difficult to retain direct carer involvement.
>
> SSD 57, North East England

> Our commitments are set out in the [name of mental health strategy document] and there is a planning group on carer involvement. There is a place on the planning group [for a carer]. However, this is currently vacant as it can be difficult to find carers with the time and inclination to be able to attend planning meetings.
>
> Health board 1, Mid-Wales

This last organisation seemed to make the assumption that carers did not want to be involved. Interestingly, when interviewed, five SSDs reported operating 'buddying' schemes to make it easier for carers to become less marginalised partners. Here buddying was taken to mean the pairing up of and support by an experienced carer with a less experienced carer. Buddying took on a concrete form in terms of support in key carers'/users' forums. Here are two notable examples of buddying, which wider evidence suggests was very successful:

> We operate a buddy scheme alongside our parent carers' training and our voucher scheme. These are our most recent and successful work with carers. The buddying makes committee roles less daunting and carers learn the ropes more quickly and with more confidence.
>
> SSD 55, South East England

> [We] have developed a project with the PCT to ensure that carers who are interested in being involved in meetings, etc, are matched with a 'buddy' carer who can accompany the carer to meetings until they are confident to attend [on their own].
>
> SSD 7, North East England

In Stage 1 of the research for this Position Paper (*see* Appendix G), carers' organisations were asked an additional question about support:

Do you give carers wishing to be involved:
* support in terms of briefings on key issues of legislation?
* support at meetings?
* opportunities to hear the views of other carers?

Over 90% of carer organisations gave a positive response to these questions.

The value of buddies to both carers and LAs was beyond question to the above organisations, and may be a route for all organisations to consider as a way of enhancing participation.

5.3.5 Reaching 'hidden' or marginalised carers

Up to this point, data has referred to levels of engagement with known carers. However, it is perfectly possible that these activities take place with little reference to traditionally marginalised carers. This is how we initially defined marginalised carers: 'People who do not recognise themselves as carers, black and ethnic minority carers, gay and lesbian carers'.

We also asked the CPRG, our review group and respondents to give other examples, and they added the following: older carers, lifetime carers, carers of people with potentially stigmatising conditions. These last include people with mental health problems, those who practise substance abuse and those who are HIV-positive or have AIDS.

To gauge levels of engagement, we asked if organisations have a written policy for including carers who are likely to be marginalised.

Table 7
Does your organisation have a written policy for including carers who are likely to be marginalised?

Organisation	Yes	No	Total
SSD	25 (39.1%)	39 (60.9%)	64 (67)
PCT	3 (27.3%)	8 (72.7%)	11 (16)
Health board	0 (0%)	1 (100%)	1 (1)
JCT	4 (50%)	4 (50%)	8 (9)
LDBP	0 (0%)	9 (100%)	9 (9)
Carers' organisation	12 (75%)	4 (25%)	16 (16)

The above findings suggest that this may be an area of weakness for organisations. The finding for PBs is particularly stark and suggests that they may assume that most family carers are known to them. Interview findings largely reflected this misapprehension. A small but active minority of SSDs, PCTs and carers' organisations, in both urban (19) and rural (2) contexts, which were engaging with BME groups (*n*=21) – for example, Turkish, Chinese, Jewish, Kurdish, Traveller and Bangladeshi communities – were at great risk of assuming that BME families 'look after their own' (120, 209, 211, 244).

In the statutory sector, there were few examples of engagement with gay and lesbian carers. This reflects Manthorpe's academic work (203), which highlights service and professional deficits in this area. Telephone interviews found the voluntary sector seemingly further ahead in this and well networked to other voluntary organisations. Organisations such as Polari, who support gay and lesbian service users, were at the forefront of this isolated support. The Alzheimer's Society Gay and Lesbian Carers Network has a worker whose job is to educate other workers in the organisation on gay and lesbian issues.

There was a paucity of activity aimed specifically at people practising substance abuse or those with stigmatised conditions or at including them more widely. Because of the significantly high number of organisations that said they did not have a policy for reaching hidden or marginalised carers, Stage 2 of the practice survey explored this issue much further. Drawing on Arnstein (152) and Goss and Miller (81), the degree of engagement with hidden or once-hidden carers varied and can be seen on a passive–active continuum as follows:

- More passive measures: paper-based measures only
  [Marginalised especially BME groups] are included in our carers strategies, although little action has been taken around the issue of gay and lesbian carers.

  SSD 42, South East England

- Mix of passive and active measures
  Our equal opportunities policy is to actively seek out hidden and marginalised carers. We do this in a variety of ways including some exciting work with GP practices. We put a 'post it' note called 'Counting on carers' on repeat prescriptions. It's *ad hoc* at the moment but we have attracted 13 of the 17 surgeries we targeted. We are currently relying on a drug company to sponsor the project....

  > Carers' centre 11, South East England

This carers' organisation adopted a novel way of using GP surgeries as awareness-raising sites. But the success of the venture relied on uncertain external funding.

- More active measures: partnership officers and funded outreach posts
  [We fund a] dedicated partnership officer, who is employed to develop the relationship between carers and the SSD ... we are using publicity fliers to attract more carers and work with GPs in surgeries to advertise the local support for carers.

  > SSD 61, North East England

One carer gave an example of limited cultural awareness resulting in an oversight in responding to hidden issues. This related not to the invisibility of the carer, where contacts with social services were significant, but the fact that assessments and provision were culturally less attuned than they could have been:

> I would describe my partner and I as culturally rather than socially marginalised. We are Jewish and find that assessments have not asked us if we have any religious or cultural beliefs. Though it is not obvious, if we were simply asked about this it would help explain why we want carers to support us flexibly and on certain days and times....
>
> Spousal carer in paid employment, caring for partner with MS,
> London borough

Frequently mentioned by 12 statutory and carer organisations were carers of children with poorly understood impairments:

> One group of carers we feel are marginalised are those of children with ADHD (Attention Deficit Hyperactivity Disorder) often seen as a 'hidden disability'. Sometimes we have to ask to meet with the director of the SSD because of the problems this particular group face. They are definitely treated as parents rather than carers.
>
> Carers' centre 10, North East England

While meeting the director may have led to desirable changes in this instance, far more preferable would have been an embedded policy for this group of parent carers. Six of the nine LDPBs mentioned ambiguities in the policy for carers of children with disabilities. Only two organisations specifically mentioned trying to reach out to carers who are in full-time or substantial employment. These statutory organisations were mindful of the impact of undertaking unpaid caring and paid employment but currently defer to voluntary sector expertise – that is, the Alzheimer's Working Carers Project.

Because of the number of organisations that did not have a policy on hidden or marginalised carers, we decided to examine this further. We analysed statutory organisations by region to see whether some regions were more likely to have evidence of written policies. Findings were diverse. In Eastern England (for regional classification, see Appendix I), 80% of respondents had a policy, but in the North East, only 25% did. However, the absence of a written policy may not be indicative of no commitment. It could be that some organisations engaged with carers before written policies were widespread. For example, as section 5.3.2 shows, the North East has been promoting carers' participation for longer than any other region.

In conclusion, it is worth noting the paradox that, despite a growing body of literature on hidden carers ($n=30/101$ literature references) and significant growth in practice awareness, there is little evidence to suggest that the problem has diminished proportionate to our growing awareness of it.

5.3.6 Agreeing outcomes and providing feedback

One might understandably assume that, once carers were involved in service planning, design, monitoring and review, a linear process of outcomes improvement would follow. The evidence from wider research counsels caution on this assumption. SCIE research (129) on involving users in planning and delivering services had suggested that organisations are involving users but are less good at defining what users expect from their involvement and then giving feedback on what difference their contribution has made (see also 65, 169, 174, 179, 226). Our questionnaire asked whether organisations defined and discussed intended outcomes of participation/involvement with carers:

Table 8
Do you agree with carers what outcomes (changes) you are looking for in the planning and delivery of services as a result of their involvement?

Organisation	Yes	No	Total
SSD	51 (86.4%)	8 (13.6%)	59 (67%)
PCT	10 (90.1%)	1 (9.1%)	11 (16%)
Health board	1 (100%)	0 (0.0)	1 (1%)
NHS trust	12 (80%)	3 (20%)	15 (16%)
JCT	6 (75%)	2 (25%)	8 (9%)
LDPB	9 (100%)	0 (0%)	9 (9%)
Carers' organisation	16 (100%)	0 (0%)	16 (0%)

We then asked whether the organisations agreed a time with carers when the outcomes would be reviewed.

Table 9
Do you agree a period of time with carers when you will review these outcomes to see whether they have been met?

Organisation	Yes	No	Total
SSD	48 (81.4%)	11 (18.6%)	59 (67%)
PCT	6 (60%)	4 (40%)	10 (16%)
Health board	0 (0%)	1 (100%)	1 (1%)
NHS trust	9 (64.3%)	5 (35.7%)	14 (16%)
JCT	5 (62.5%)	3 (37.5%)	8 (9%)
LDPB	5 (55%)	4 (45%)	9 (9%)
Carers' organisation	11 (69%)	3 (19%)	14 (16%)

One interesting conclusion from these two sets of data is that, although all LDPBs said that they agreed outcomes with carers, they did not agree time frames for reviewing them. Therefore one must question whether there is a gap between rhetoric and reality here. The above findings do, however, suggest that SSDs are trying to get feedback from, and provide feedback to, a wide audience of carers.

Methods for receiving feedback varied. Most of the LAs (*n*=48) talked about questionnaires (postal and administered):

> Our carers work is still forming up and not without its difficulty ... but we have begun to canvass the opinion of carers and we have a high level of commitment to making carers' participation happen.... For example, we have responded to carers' comments by having an induction programme for professionals working with carers to raise the issues.
>
> Health board 1, Northern Ireland

Overall, feedback was sought in the majority of LAs through questionnaires. Although potentially valuable as a planning tool, these approaches alone are likely to meet only a threshold standard of carer participation as research agendas are often set before questionnaires are designed and despatched. A few (*n*=3) authorities used both formalised methods of canvassing views (questionnaires) and visits to carers' forums. One SSD showed a clear audit mechanism for getting and acting on feedback:

> Carer feedback is taken both collectively and individually. The views are fed into the service improvement workbook. Each business unit has to get that feedback and act on it. It is monitored by the Business Improvement Unit.
>
> SSD 17, English Midlands

Another SSD used creative ways of arriving at more candid views from carers:

> We have found that more informal days, such as the provision of alternative therapies, swimming, etc, have proved more useful in gaining the views of carers rather than formal meetings....
>
> SSD 52, Central Wales

Likewise most statutory organisations believe that they provide carers with feedback on the effect that their involvement has had on service planning and delivery:

Table 10
As a result of carer involvement, do you provide carers with feedback on how their input has changed services?

Organisation	Yes	No	Total
SSD	57 (91.9%)	5 (8.1%)	62 (67%)
PCT	10 (90.9%)	1 (9.1%)	11 (16%)
Health board	0 (0%)	1 (100%)	1 (1%)
NHS trust	10 (83.0%)	2 (16.7%)	12 (16%)
JCT	5 (83.3%)	1 (16.7%)	6 (9%)
LDPB	9 (100%)	0	9 (9%)

Follow-up interviews showed that much feedback from SSDs, in particular, was via the traditional written route of newsletters:

> The carers strategy ... is presented to the carers' coordination partnership for comments and amendments to ensure all partners' views are taken into account. This group includes carer representatives.... A newsletter reaches all carers on our database. The newsletter includes an update on each service area, plus a report on the carers' coordinating partnership.
>
> SSD 32, English Midlands

What was of more interest was whether organisations themselves could give evidence of how carer involvement had changed service planning and delivery:

> Although in LD services we are still in the early stages of a comprehensive approach to carers.... We are starting to see real gains and real partnership working via design meetings, how meetings are run and how to provide good accessible forms of communication and information for carers.
>
> SSD 63, North West England

> [Carer participation] has raised the carer profile, made our service more personal and having a bigger impact. It helps put different perspectives on management and partners' agendas.
>
> SSD 9, North East England

The occupational therapy service was recently reorganised in part in response to concerns and comments from users and carers. Access to the service changed from 'paper-based' [a long and complicated self-referral form, however small the piece of equipment required] to 'phone-based' access, enabling the service user/carer to explain their need and have it met quickly where small items only are required.

SSD 17, English Midlands

Facilitation of a borough-wide and regular carers' support group allows carers to be vocal and assertive when influencing the planning and delivery of services ... this has also made a positive impact in the improvement of current services.

Carers' centre and carer 13, South East England

Some SSDs provided very specific examples of positive outcomes, this time for professionals. The example below is from a largely unfavourable funding and cross-statutory partnership environment. Nevertheless, feedback was felt to be beneficial to carers:

The carers' support post was a direct result of carers' input as they felt more was needed for carers in [name of area]. So the service wouldn't exist without carers and the work is very useful....

SSD 66, South Wales

Some examples of making a difference were in response to the persistence of carers, but nonetheless led to substantive changes:

... The local authority sneaked in the decision – which goes against the Crossroads model – that carers could not bank their hours If, for some reason or another, Crossroads could not offer the service that particular day. I just went ballistic. I phoned the local councillor and she got in touch with the team manager or whatever and, yes, now carers across the board can bank their hours....

Lifetime carer of daughter with learning difficulty, English Midlands

There've been lots of opportunities to have a say about what I want and that makes a change. Staff are more aware of carers' needs, and I work with the local carers strategy group and learning disabilities board [LDPB]. We have our say and they get written responses back telling us what they have done about it.

Lifetime carer for son who is blind and has a learning difficulty, North East England

Health trusts and PCTs could also cite examples of making a difference albeit their focus was on enhancing carers' awareness of health conditions or treatment regimes:

We have worked a lot with carers to raise awareness and skills – for example, falls in the elderly. We developed a comprehensive falls prevention pack to every 'at risk' patient following concerns expressed by carers.

NHS Trust 7, Eastern England

Training is now provided for carers of heart patients In cardiac resuscitation.... We are also much more flexible with our visiting times where carers are concerned.

Acute hospitals trust 14, North East England

Carer involvement was also seen to aid health professionals in working with carers:

> Carer involvement in the NSF for older people has increased our awareness of carer issues and led to the development of the volunteer policy which includes provision for extra respite care for carers attending meetings.
>
> PCT 3, Pennines

Some responses were short, but suggested a general building of partnership and exchange of ideas in carer participation:

> Involvement on any meaningful level has been fairly recent. This has, however, generated positive feedback. Carers are now saying that they feel more listened to and that they can see positive changes.
>
> SSD 26, North East England

One LA emphasised the benefits of carer participation in terms of the organisational and personal insights gained from working with carers:

> It has widened our knowledge and understanding of the carers' experience and pathway. Recognition and understanding of carers and their role is much more widely understood in the organisation.
>
> SSD 24, London borough

Other examples simply represent evidence of authorities listening to carers and effecting change:

> Included in the joint carers' strategy is feedback on the comments received from carers over the previous two or three years, summarised under 10 themes, that underpinned the development of a carers strategy action plan. Examples include carer health and manual handling support and information to improve the health of carers so that the caring relationship [is] maintained.
>
> SSD 62, London borough

While the latter detailed the feedback process beginning with carer comments, examples were also given of more LA-driven feedback – for example, in disseminating research findings:

> We identified the need to understand better how well our respite service was functioning for carers and users alike. Part of our current research on quality of respite care includes feedback to carers.
>
> SSD 22, North East England

Similarly respondents were asked to detail how carer involvement has made a positive difference to the support of carers:

> Carers identified their main priority was the facility to take short breaks which were controlled by themselves – a flexible, easy-to-operate scheme with maximum choice, giving as much enjoyment to the carer as possible. Our voucher

scheme was developed which provides all of this and we won a Health and Social Care Award.

SSD 35, North West England

Carers' views have had some impact on our increased respite service, and we have also revised our assessment pro forma to reflect these views.

SSD 55, Eastern England

Perhaps the greatest evidence for the commitment to sharing power and involving carers is where substantial policy change is made, as the following suggests:

We were taking some flak from carers who needed funding and breaks and decided to undertake consultation about charging for respite services. Priorities and clear messages came out of this process, and the council decided to drop all charges for respite are. Money is now taken from the Carers Grant.

SSD 67, London borough

Many of the above examples are important if rather passive examples of carer involvement that equate to Arnstein's second level of participation, that of 'tokenism' (152). The final example, however, more squarely sits within Arnstein's highest range of involvement, which he dubbed 'citizen power'.

By responding to direct pressure from carers and building their views into overall respite care planning (rather than simply confining them to the details or just carrying out passive consultation), the SSD began the process of power sharing (4, 77, 80, 136, 138).

Positive feedback arrangements based on an iterative process (that is, exchange and development of ideas) was mentioned in diverse ways by only four out of 15 carer respondents. The following captures well this general perception of a feedback process operating to enhance carers' lives:

We have the opportunity to have our say and this is acted on. We have an ongoing dialogue and annual reviews with social services and day centre staff. My daughter and I both have an active say, and I would say it does get noticed.

Older male parent carer for daughter with a learning difficulty, English Midlands

5.3.7 Accountability

The above examples suggest good practice in feeding back to carers who are able to be involved, at a strategic level. It does not account for the vast majority of carers who are not. Respondents were asked: 'Do you ensure that groups of carers can influence policy that is accountable to other carers?'.

Table 11
Do you ensure that groups of carers can influence policy in a way that is accountable to other carers?

Organisation	Yes	No	Total
SSD	56 (86.2%)	9 (13.8%)	65 (67%)
PCT	9 (75%)	3 (25%)	12 (16%)
Health board	1 (100%)	0 (0%)	1 (1%)
NHS trust	11 (73.3%)	4 (26.7%)	15 (16%)
JCT	6 (75%)	2 (25%)	8 (9%)
LDPB	7 (78%)	2 (22%)	9 (9%)
Carers' organisation	11 (69%)	5 (31%)	16 (16%)

It was interesting that a number of those who answered 'yes' could not (or would not) say how accountability worked. But to be fair, most organisations did recognise the problem of providing evidence of accountability:

> We struggle hard to ensure that carers are accountable to other carers. We have a 'carers shadow group' not involved in the various boards and decision-making processes. We encourage the LD partnership board to talk to the shadow groups at away days. Some people don't find this as onerous as being a full board member, but we recognised it may not be accountable to all those carers who aren't involved.
>
> Carers' centre 11, South East England

> Carers find it hard to represent anyone other than themselves. Every individual has too many issues to be worried about someone else.
>
> SSD 3, Eastern England

Others were more satisfied about structures of accountability:

> Carer representatives on the partnership board are accountable to local groups of carers. Reps are elected by postal ballot of local carers.
>
> LDPB 2, English Midlands

There were also a few examples of ensuring accountability given by statutory organisations:

Feedback

This medium-sized unitary authority in the English Midlands identifies carer participation as a lead issue in the modernisation of its services, including the use and reporting of feedback. It takes carer comments and then aims to feed back to a wide constituency of carers. This may then overcome the limits of relying on a small number of committed individuals who are seen as 'committee carers', who may be less effective in feeding back to the wider body of carers.

One example provided by this authority involved carers being asked to help in a review of respite care. Multiple contact methods were used to invite carers to a review forum, and a small number put themselves forward to be involved. This allowed a clear focus on the issues, but resulted in a range of perspectives. The agenda was not firmly set at the outset, although some clear statutory and budgetary factors impacted the nature and scope of the review.

The decisions and direction of the review group were much more comprehensive because of its contact with the wider carer constituency through carer links with support groups, paper questionnaires, shopping mall exercises and a 'check back' session with carers. The team of carers on the review forum fed back the results to the wider body of carers via a presentation, to which all carers who had commented or took part in the review were invited. This brought carers and councillors together and allowed carers to hear and comment on council deliberations.

Feedback from carers on the whole process and outcomes of the service review were largely positive and ultimately played an integral part in the reshaping of services.

SSD 11, English Midlands

This authority had tried to ensure accountability on a single issue. Recognising the diversity of carers and the range of carer issues, the issue of accountability is perhaps one organisation's need to reflect on and share good practice with more. Olsen, Parker and Drewett's important account (184) of the challenge of linking strategic and street-level accountability is very pertinent here. There is also a need to be aware that not all carers are involved in networks that respond to efforts to ensure accountability. Something that is not always the case as witnessed by the numbers who do not seek out hidden and marginalised carers.

5.3.8 Carers' assessments

Thus far, the research findings have been about carers' involvement at a strategic level. The researchers also wanted to try and look at carers' involvement and participation in assessment – first, at a strategic level in planning the content and process of assessment documentation, and second, to discover what impact individual carers might have on their own assessment process.

Table 12
Does your organisation seek carer feedback on the content and process of carer assessments (at both a strategic and an individual level)?

Organisation	Yes	No	Total
SSD	43 (68.3%)	20 (31.7%)	63 (67%)
PCT	1 (20%)	4 (80%)	5 (12%)
JCT	6 (67%)	3 (33%)	9 (9%)
Health board	0 (0%)	1 (100%)	1 (1%)
NHS trust	6 (75%)	2 (25%)	8 (16%)
LDPB	6 (67%)	3 (33%)	9 (9%)

NB: It was assumed by the researchers at the questionnaire stage that carers' organisations would not carry out assessments, although surprisingly the questionnaires revealed that six out of 16 carers organisations (37.5%) were carrying them out.

The results then are more equivocal than might have been expected, and the telephone interviews add to the conclusion that carer assessments may be an area of relative weakness in carer participation terms. They are clearly an important part of both the statutory process of establishing needs and a key plank of supportive provision for carers.

Few organisations (*n*=four) mentioned trying to involve carers at a strategic level to determine both the content and the process of assessments. But there were some good examples:

> We wanted carers to take a lead [in assessments]. Carers felt that what went into carer assessments was vital.... They liked the package from [national mental health organisation] who have done a lot of work on carer assessments.... Carers liked the way questions were framed. However, this didn't fit with the [name of organisation's] care assessment process. I know this was wrong but it does take time to bring all organisations on board, particularly health. In the end, we fronted the design but brought in the ideas that would work and the assessment form and process were written by carers.... It is easier to do it yourself, but you have got to hold back if you want carers to be true partners.
>
> JCT 8, North East England

Comments like the following were isolated but significant:

> We don't feel we are performing as well as we should be. Carers have refused to be part of a force to change assessments. They feel this is something that should be left to the individual carer.
>
> LDPB 2, English Midlands

There is perhaps an assumption in this second comment that carers have more power in influencing their individual assessments than this research suggests they do. Although the first organisation above was unable to take all elements of carer views and suggestions on board when redesigning the assessment process, they did engage with an iterative process with carers, mentioning limited time availability as a determining factor in fully involving carers. This level of involvement in designing assessments was rarely mentioned, although some authorities did canvass carers' views:

> We have conducted a big review of carer assessment seeking the views of carers. We found that carers did not want to 'tick boxes' but wanted a dialogue about their involvement, that the validation of their work was one of the most important criteria in assessment.
>
> SSD 49, Eastern England

Involvement at an individual level was explored in the telephone interviews, which resulted in a much less optimistic picture. Indeed, some carers seem unaware of their right to an assessment, while others were unaware that they had had one.

> In our survey [of carer experiences and perceptions], we established that 66% of carers who responded had not been given an assessment of their needs of those that were assessed, 46% did not receive a copy of their assessment document. We are getting there with establishing the importance of it [CP], but there is evidence of tokenism and perversely we feel the recent White Paper on Adult Social Care [actually the proposed Green Paper] takes senior managers further away from carers [quoted verbatim].
>
> Carers' centre 1 and carer, English Midlands

This above example reflects the findings of a number of studies of carer assessment, which point up the continued uncertainty and lack of clarity that sometimes attach to assessment rights, despite myriad policy pronouncements about the importance of assessments for informal carers (68, 102, 155, 173, 179, 200, 208). Some carers noted that they had not had any feedback from their assessment and, in a few instances, had never heard back from social services or their health professional.

Four LAs were explicit about the ways in which they had tried to enhance the assessment process or simply raise carers' awareness of their entitlement to assessments. Some organisations mentioned that carers were suspicious or wary of statutory bodies undertaking assessments, preferring carers' or other voluntary sector organisations to appraise their needs in the first instance. However, there was a degree of uncertainty and indeed muddle as to just how far (if at all) LAs could devolve their carer assessments.

The clearest evidence of certainty about assessments came from the following:

> For carer assessment, we used an advisory group of eight carers and 14 social workers to research views of carers; these [are] fed into revised assessments.... We cannot devolve the actual assessment responsibility ... to the voluntary sector;

but I would acknowledge the possible misunderstandings that lie in the PI and RAP guidance.

SSD 5, Eastern England

Other respondents expressed a degree of uncertainty and muddle about this issue:

We have recently reviewed carer assessments through the Carers' Forum. We conduct assessments through the local carers' organisations if carers do not want to be involved with the social services. If the carers' organisation requires resources from the LA [at Stage 3 of the assessment], then this part of the assessment is transferred to the LA.

SSD 49, Eastern England

Clearly a compromise is being struck here – that is, adopting a flexible, perhaps less daunting approach to assessment. This statement begs the question as to whether LAs have the power to devolve assessment. This is again shown in the example below:

We are updating the carer assessment documentation with the involvement of carers. We do our own [SSD] assessments, yes, but about 40-45% of the Carers Grant goes to voluntary organisations and some of this will fund assessments; but this may prove difficult with new performance indicators.

SSD 53, English Midlands

The latest guidance from the DH can give carers' organisations service-level agreements to do carer assessment. This is poor practice, we feel, because it keeps carers 'out there' instead of working with us in an integrated way....

SSD 18, London borough

The starkest example of confusion as to the 'right way' to approach carer assessment in applying a carers-first philosophy is evident in the next response. The comments come from an innovative and very carer-focused centre:

We would love to do carer assessments more fully. We do some work on assessment with young carers, but adults ... we did have a foray into assessment of adults, alongside direct service provision with the local BME carer community [but] we ended up in court over equal opportunities issues. So we do want to do more and have carers at the centre of that process, but we feel we need tighter guidance just what we can and cannot do....

Carers' centre 6, South East England

Perhaps the best example of compromise and flexibility was this:

Social services and the carers' centre give out a carers' pack. In this is a request to have a carer assessment. The [carer coordinator] helps individual carers fill in this form and ... the council have a commitment to respond to this request [for form completion support] within 48 hours.

SSD 59, North West England

Overall, carer assessment was one of the least consistent and least satisfactory elements of carer participation according to statutory agencies and carers. There is clearly a need for definitive guidance around assessments, given their importance in supporting carers generally in their caring roles and specifically in their increased participation in care planning. The question of what is and what is not reasonable for LAs to encourage carers and carers' centres to do is very important. The following was typical of the limits to assessment in many LAs:

> We do enter into assessments as we are guided to do, but [LA name] have not taken full account of carers to date and some do slip through, whilst others may simply not know they have been assessed as it was done as part of the user's assessment. The clarity with which we offer assessments to carers could be improved.
>
> SSD 19, London borough

Working at an individual level with carers is where the partnerships most seem to break down:

> We give our input, but we don't really influence the way they [SSDs] work. For example, I have commented on the need to have more choice of agency staff, but my ideas have not led to any greater control....
>
> Older BME carer for daughter with physical impairments, London

Some of the most critical comments came from the following carer who points to shortcomings in both macro-level policy and street-level practice:

> We have a real problem here. When you ask for anything, you are told that funds are limited or circumstances are not serious enough to warrant support. There is some commitment on behalf of social services, but some don't want to know about carers. The message is: 'We have enough on our plate....'
>
> Spousal carer for wife with mental health problems, North Wales

This sentiment is borne out by corroborative evidence:

> Decisions, because of resources, often have to be made in relation to identified priorities, and although we consult with carers and hear their views, the development of services may be influenced by other priorities. What is important is that carers are made aware of why decisions are made.
>
> SSD 4, South Wales

> I don't think I can influence them [SSD] but you can sometimes get an answer to a difficult situation. They either say, 'You can pursue this if you want to go ahead' or 'You can try but we don't think you will get anywhere'. So when you say 'influence them' ....
>
> BME carer of mother with chronic illnesses, London borough

> I was told my [carer] assessment would be reviewed, [but] in practice review doesn't happen. [We] should just be able to ring in and say I need a review....
> We have badgered the local authority to get what we want, and have very much

altered the service to us specifically, but not to the way they [SSD] work generally, the level of service.

> Spousal carer for partner with MS, London borough

I was promised a lot of things, that they [social worker] would contact Age Concern and I have heard nothing despite follow-up calls.... I have learnt that it is easier to try to do things for yourself.

> Older spousal carer for wife with chronic health problems, English Midlands

Sometimes carers were able to make their voices heard about their own individual experiences, as the following two examples show:

I was dissatisfied with the level of care that was being provided for my son when he was first in hospital and then subsequently discharged.... [I] complained initially to [name] health trust and then to the mental health commissioner and eventually we started having a dialogue with somebody quite senior who then arranged for my son to be transferred from the local [mental health] team that covered the rural area to the town where I live and we both get a much higher level of attention. [Name of carers' centre] with the help of social and health services have created seven carer support worker posts and the centre works closely with the local community mental health team....

> Parent carer for son with mental health problems, English Midlands

My participation has definitely made a difference. We have the final say in which agency provides for my son; we have regular meetings with the director of social services and our discussion with them led to money for our 'pamper room' at the [carers'] centre.

> Older carer for son with head injury, North East England

It might be argued, however, that even though these carers were able to make an impact on their own situations, and those of others, they were only able to do so because of their high level of personal involvement in the strategic process. This is not the case for the vast majority of carers, who rely on established systems and processes.

5.3.9 Financial constraints

Scarcity of resources was commonly cited by carers, carers' centre staff and statutory professionals as one of the main reasons for lack of involvement at the individual carer level. The most common points from carers related to difficulty getting hold of social work staff except in emergencies or after prolonged efforts. The second most significant problem mentioned was resources:

We do our level best to involve carers in all that we do. We have been partially successful, but we are so hard pressed and social workers have massive case loads here. We try to work with the local carers' centre, but the process usually starts with a crisis and the involvement of social services.

> SSD 36, South West England

We have lots of good will, but we don't have a lot of money for this [carer participation] or more concrete support. For example, there is little for those who care for [the] chronically sick, but rehabilitation and mental health have had carer issues out there for some years....

NHS trust 15, South Wales

However, a more cynical view came from one carers' organisation:

A carer died last year and left money to deliver more flexible and creative services to carers. But the statutory teams weren't that excited. They were frightened to do more assessments because they thought it would lead to more demand that couldn't be met....

Carers' centre 8, South East England

5.3.10 Training of staff in carer participation and involvement

It might be expected that one important way to ensure carer involvement at all levels of an organisation would be through training staff in participatory approaches. Stage 1 of our research revealed the following:

Table 13
Do your employees receive training in carer involvement/inclusion?

Organisation	Yes	No	Total
SSD	50 (75.8%)	16 (24.2%)	66 (67%)
PCT	8 (66.7%)	4 (33.3%)	12 (16%)
Health board	0 (0%)	1 (100%)	1 (1%)
NHS trust	10 (66.7%)	5 (33.3%)	15 (16%)
JCT	7 (87.5%)	1 (12.5%)	8 (9%)
LDPB	9 (100%)	0 (100%)	9 (9%)

Most SSDs (75.8%) say that they are undertaking training in carer participation. The groups most likely to be offered such training are social workers and OTs. This is surprising in view of the difficulties with assessments that carers face at street level, although the problems may have been more to do with the need to control resources at that level (99) than a fundamental antagonism towards involvement. Carer coordinators and managers, especially in PCT and NHS trust settings, were often the most comprehensively briefed in participation issues, often via routes such as the 'Expert Patient Programme', public–patient involvement working or partnership board experiences. This reflects the preponderance of training or education articles in the healthcare (153, 163, 191, 213, 224, 237) rather than in the social services arena (215, 216).

Telephone interviews elicited the extent and nature of training, which varied immensely. At one extreme, a few SSDs were providing general training about carers, which made no specific mention of carer involvement.

There is no separate course on carer involvement but the issue is included in carers awareness training. This interagency training has been attended by over 1,200 people.

SSD 42, South East England

More commonly, carer involvement training was delivered only to specific levels of care workers or to professionals working with specific groups:

• Targeted approaches to training in involvement and participation
Here, targeted training in carer participation took two main forms: targeting of particular user groups and the targeting of certain identified staff. First, different user groups:

We do carer involvement training, but only with mental health services staff. They have always been a priority group in fulfilling the NSF remit.

SSD 20, English Midlands

Employees receive training in carer involvement via person-centred planning training in LD services through regular sessions in older people's services including SAP training.

SSD 63, North West England

Not all workers receive training: new social workers have induction, [and] other staff are aware of changes in legislation and the development of carers' services. New legislation will increase the need for staff training.

SSD 14, South East England

• A broader range of training
In this category, the variation in perceived need to deliver training in carer participation was reflected in the different profiles of staff receiving such training:

We deliver training to social workers, community care workers, team managers, service managers and occupational therapists.

SSD 54, South East England

We currently train all our social care staff. This will change imminently and then include all workers who come into contact with carers – for example, district nurses....

SSD 39, Eastern England

Some LAs provide carer involvement training to an unexpected range of recipients. This example reflects involvement of more strategic staff who influence the care planning decisions:

At the moment, we are giving carer training, [which] focuses on their input to services, to care and service managers, councillors and departmental teams.

SSD 7, Southern England

Other responses were somewhat contradictory in claiming coverage and then specifying the boundaries of their training:

> All social work teams receive training in this area: mental health staff, older people and children [sic].
>
> SSD 59, North West England

Other responses provided evidence of a rapid expansion of carer participation training activity:

> Social work and care staff at induction receive training and in their NVQs [national vocational qualifications]. We are currently planning to equip carers to become involved in staff training and selection....
>
> SSD 9, North East England

> It is our intention to include carers on all planning forums. This has proved easier for some workers than for others ...
>
> SSD 22, North East England

> [Carer involvement] ... has changed the way I work, but now we have to change the whole LA culture so that users and carers are always involved in improving and developing services – some specialisms are much more advanced in this work than others.
>
> SSD 6, Eastern England

- Best practice in training

Examples of best practice saw successful involvement of carers in sharing with professionals their perspective as carers, and in changing policy and practice. These equate to higher-level participation as outlined by Arnstein (152), Goss and Miller (81) and, most recently, the Audit Commission (51). This is illustrated in the following:

> Feedback from staff re: training suggests their practice will change as a result of carers' input.... Production of [a] carers' guide/pathway demonstrates commitment of both health and social services. The funding of the carers' centre is a direct result of discussions between the director of social services and carers.
>
> SSD 51, North West England

The most effective training was seen as validating carers' experiences and helpful for workers in gaining carer insights. First, carer feedback:

> We include carer feedback in our training. We have many positive quotes from carers stating how the [staff] training 'has changed my life'.
>
> SSD 49, Eastern England

and on direct carer involvement in training:

> The borough provide two types of training – awareness training aimed at professionals, which covered a whole day and included carer assessment and

involving carers. [A carers' organisation] ran the session. [The] second type [is] for carers, run by the professional carers' forum, a day event to share information through workshops and discussion.

> SSD 50, London borough

and on impact:

> The feedback we get from staff re training suggests their practice will change as a result of carer input....

> SSD 41, North East England

Some examples might suggest that explicit mention of carer involvement is not always necessary where carers' voices feature in training. The following LA answered 'No' to the question: 'Do your employees receive training in carer involvement, inclusion, participation?'.

> No, but we do involve carers and carers' organisations directly in training for social workers and carers' issues.

> SSD 32, South West England

The extent of carer involvement in training was not made clear in this example. Indeed, one notable feature of commentaries on training and carer involvement was the lack of outcomes appraisal of such training. The extent to which such training makes a difference to working with carers and the carer experience remains uncertain in most instances.

The groups least likely to receive training were polarised and included entry-level care workers – for example, home care staff – at one extreme and hospital doctors and acute para-medical staff at the other. GP engagement with carer issues was beginning to happen in certain localities where financial incentives to identify carers were mainstreamed into GP practices.

Two other main themes came out of the telephone interviews that had not been incorporated in the questionnaires. These were 'emergency planning' and 'sharing good practice'.

5.3.11 Emergency planning

It was felt by the 'lifetime carers' contributing to the research protocol that one of the main reasons for needing to contact social services, particularly for older carers, was the need to know that the person cared for would be taken care of if anything happened to the carer. This was seen as particularly pertinent for carers of people with learning difficulties. LDPBs' respondents were therefore asked: 'Does your board have a written policy for older carers?' and 'Does your board have a policy for emergency planning for carers?'. Surprisingly, only two out of nine LDPBs had a policy for one or both. The issue was of such concern to the carer researchers that it was decided to pursue this question further with all SSDs interviewed.

Practice among the organisations interviewed was very varied, but can be summarised as *ad hoc* and largely triggered by acute health problems of the carer or rapid but planned hospital discharge of service users. For example, there was little evidence of systematic cross-service protocols for responding to the death of a carer except where *Valuing people* (90) had influenced SSDs to introduce emergency planning for carers of people with learning difficulties.

There are scant references to emergency planning in the carer literature, although Carers UK have explored the issue in a very recent report (241). This focuses largely on acute or short-term health emergencies rather than the total loss of a carer. Other comments suggested improvements had been made but were not supported by substantive evidence of the process or outcome. The question of emergency planning, often referred to by carers as the 'what if' dilemma, has yet to percolate into carer participation dialogue and, indeed, practice. The following is an example of best practice in emergency planning.

> As regards emergency planning, our carers strategy includes health input and better emergency planning at the initial carer assessment point. We aim to be proactive rather than reactive. How successful this is in practice is too early to tell....
>
> SSD 19, London borough

Useful, but more perhaps passive measures were evident in the following quote:

> Yes, [emergency planning] has been a major point from consultation. Assessments include telephone numbers [for use] in an emergency. The council are trying to integrate the use of the existing [user] careline which vulnerable people can use in an emergency....
>
> SSD 67, London borough

The above, in concentrating on making carers get in contact with social services, says little about the mechanisms that would then be used to respond to the substantive needs occasioned by the death or serious illness of a carer and builds on a service user model of service participation. The next example also discusses good preliminary gestures, but is a far-from-complete arrangement for emergency planning:

> This [EP] is a requirement of the Welsh Assembly's unified assessment process. Regular staff training takes place to ensure this happens. We are currently trying to get funding to initiate the 'Emergency Card for Carers' to be offered through the [organisation name]. This is a system where a central agency holds details of a carer's support ... network and agencies involved [with the carer].... We are finding it hard to get funding as we are not funding 'outcomes' but funding 'peace of mind for carers'....
>
> SSD 52, Mid Wales

Despite claims of integrated assessment schemes, user rather than carer emergency planning had primacy in practice terms:

Not everyone covers this [emergency planning] contingency. The emergency planning tends to be included in the service user's assessment rather than the carer's.

SSD 29, Southern England

Some LA respondents simply did not connect with the 'what if', death-of-carer notion and clearly did not have a service vocabulary for it:

> ... not sure what's included, but the council are in close contact with [name of rehabilitation service], a multi-disciplinary team which intervenes in an emergency. The team offer quick respite to prevent hospital admission.

SSD 59, North West England

5.3.12 Sharing and developing good practice

One key concern that was raised by professionals interviewed was that of sharing good practice. This issue only came out of the second phase of the practice survey (that is, the interviews); therefore comments are few but nonetheless are fairly consistent. This also reflects the paucity of academic articles on sharing practice, with most research focusing on intraprofessional (153, 166, 169, 170) or interprofessional (155, 167) sharing for *ad hoc* purposes rather than the wholesale roll-out of best practice. This may be explained by the absence of consensus as to best practice, with LAs being concerned not to embrace practice that quickly becomes outdated.

The key message was that active regional consortia with carer involvement were helpful in providing ideas and innovations. Here is a range of comments:

> We [the LA] belong to the London Carers Working Forum. Quarterly meetings are held to share good practice These are invaluable in developing services – eg [this was how we] developed a cross-borough protocol for carer assessments....

SSD 67, London borough

> We have a Southern Area Network meeting. This includes statutory and voluntary sectors. We are disappointed about the ability to engage the PCT. They have a representative at the Network, but different priorities often make things difficult.

SSD 29, Southern England

> [We are] involved in [the] lead officer group for the North West of England, and attend their quarterly meetings. We attended the annual conference: the Carers into Employment Initiative. Have visited different local authorities around the country to share good practice. We use the Internet and local carers' network also....

SSD 59, North West England

The following felt that national support and role models were needed:

> We are working really flat out to make it [carer participation] work. We have problems making the carers' group work and have difficulties with our PCTs in the area, getting them on board. Role models are wanted as we simply cannot make things work 'from scratch'....
>
> SSD 41, North East England

> We have a regional service user and carer involvement forum across the [geographical area], so we do share practice, but within a region we risk getting inward-looking and all copying less-than-ideal practice. We need a national website spreading good practice.
>
> SSD 33, South West England

and most telling:

> At the time we needed more guidance, I think the wrong message [was] given out with the loss of the lead carer role at the DH. We saw that as very symbolic....
>
> SSD 6, Eastern England

6 Concluding comments

This survey seems to indicate that, strategically, statutory organisations are trying to involve and include carers and feeding back what a difference that involvement has made. The situation for individual carers, whether known to organisations or not, is much less optimistic. Staff and carers from the Sunderland Carers' Centre comment below on why they think this is the case.

It is our view that some of the major problems arise when practitioners try to turn forward-looking strategies for involving carers into practice. Many practitioners still wrestle with the performance management culture that, in our view, still results in assessments being output- rather than outcome-led – that is, using numbers rather than quality-of-life criteria. Carer assessments particularly challenge the traditional mind-set, as the support provided often needs to be very individually focused. For instance, the deadlines by which assessments have to be completed may not give carers time to think through what they need, especially if they do not see themselves as carers. The sharing of power – an issue so central to substantive carer, user and professional relations – seems unlikely in such a service climate.

The examples given throughout this Position Paper have suggested that single assessment process documentation and 'user-friendly' solutions may go against carer-friendly carer assessments. Time is usually of the essence to carers – particularly where guilt about limited time commitment may be a factor– and time is in short supply for busy practitioners, too. Carers often need to think about which services are going to help them as carers and, at the same time, they don't want to service users. Carers have to become comfortable about accepting support, and assessments may need to be done over several visits.

Unless carer awareness and carer issues and outcomes – other than the total number of assessments (outputs) – are taking into account in assessing performance, involving individual carers is likely to remain a vision rather than a reality. There is also some local evidence that training for practitioners may become disconnected from everyday work, which is why we asked the question about training and involving carers rather than training *per se*. Our view is that training for practitioners is more effective if presented by carers as problem-solving exercises about their actual experiences, rather than training in how to do paper-based assessments.

There are many examples of good practice detailed above, but one wonders whether these are in spite of rather than because of wider service conditions. The degree to which best practice can be replicated remains to be seen. Yet we have seen that consultation-only methods are likely to advance carer participation little.

It is hoped that the above survey will contribute, however modestly, to a progressive momentum for best practice to be shared in a climate that affords carers and practitioners full scope to realise their aims. Power sharing must lie at the heart of such a progressive shift to the fullest carer participation.

References

1   Zarb, G. (1992) 'On the road to Damascus: First steps towards changing the social relations of production', *Disability, Handicap and Society*, vol 7, no 2, pp 125-131.

2   Kemshall, H. and Littlechild, R. (eds) (2000) *User involvement and participation in social care: Research informing practice*, London: Jessica Kingsley Publishing.

3   Adams, R. (2002) *Social policy and social work*, London: Palgrave.

4   Jack, R. (1996) *Empowerment in community care*, London: Chapman Hall.

5   Oliver, M. (1992) 'Changing the social relations of research production', *Disability, Handicap and Society*, vol 7, no 2, pp 101-14.

6   Toronto Group (2005) *Research as empowerment? A series of seminars organised by the Toronto Group.* York: Joseph Rowntree Foundation/York Publishing Services.

7   Carers UK (2001) *It could be you – the chances of becoming a carer*, London: Carers UK.

8   Department of Health (1999) *Caring about carers: A national strategy for carers*, London: DH.

9   George, M. (2001) *It could be you: A report on the chances of becoming a carer*, London: Carers UK.

10   Hirst, M. (2001) 'Trends in informal care in Great Britain during the 1990s', *Health and Social Care in the Community*, vol 9, no 6, pp 348-357.

11   Nolan, M., Grant, G. and Keady, J. (1996) *Understanding family care: A multidisciplinary model of caring and coping*, Buckingham: Open University Press.

12   Parker, G. and Lawton, D. (1994) *Different types of care, different types of carer: Evidence from the General Household Survey*, London: HMSO.

13   Rowlands, O. and Parker, G. (1998) *Informal carers: Results of an independent study carried out by the Office for National Statistics*, London: Office for National Statistics.

14   Gordon, D., Adelman, L., Ashworth, K., Bradshaw, J., Levitas, R., Middelton, S., Pantazis, S., Patsios, D., Payne, S., Townsend, P. and Williams, J. (2000) *Poverty and social exclusion in Britain*, York: Joseph Rowntree Foundation/York Publishing Services.

15   Carers National Association (2000) *Caring on the breadline*, London: Carers National Association.

16   Department of Health (1998) *Modernising social services: Promoting independence, improving protection, raising standards*, London: DH.

17   Department of Social Security (1999) *Opportunity for all: Tackling poverty and social exclusion – first annual report to Parliament*, London: TSO.

18   Stalker, K. (2003) *Reconceptualising work with carers: New directions for policy and practice*, London: Jessica Kingsley Publishing.

19   Glendinning, C. (1992) *The costs of informal care: Looking inside the household*, London: HMSO.

20   Holzhauzen, E. and Pearlman, V. (2000) *Caring on the breadline – The financial implications of caring*, London: Carers National Association.

21   Howard, M. (2001) *Paying the price: Carers, poverty and social exclusion*, London: Child Poverty Action Group.

22   Chamba, R., Waqar, A., Hirst, M., Lawton, D. and Beresford, B. (1999) *On the edge: Minority ethnic families caring for a severely disabled child*, York/Bristol: Joseph Rowntree Foundation/The Policy Press.

23   Social Exclusion Unit (2000) *Minority ethnic issues in social exclusion and neighbourhood renewal*, London: Cabinet Office.

24   Ward, L. (2001) *Family matters: Counting families in*, London: DH.

25   Fisher, M. (1994) 'Man-made care: Community care and older male carers', *British Journal of Social Work*, no 24 pp 659-80.

26   Gunaratnam, Y. (1997) 'Breaking the silence: Black and minority ethnic carers and service provision', in J. Bornat, J. Johnson, C. Pereira, D. Pilgrim and F. Williams (eds) *Community care: A reader*, Basingstoke: Macmillan.

27   Philpot, T. and Ward, L. (eds) **(1995?)** *Values and visions: Changing ideas in services for people with learning difficulties*, Oxford: Butterworth Heinemann.

28   Butt, J. (1994) *Same service or equal service? The second report on Social Service Department's development, implementation and monitoring of services for black and minority ethnic communities*, London: DH/HMSO.

29   Butt, J. and Box, L. (1997) *Supportive services, effective strategies: The views of black-led organisations and the social care agencies on the nature of social care for black communities*, London: Race Equality Unit.

30   Ahmad, W. and Jones, L. (1998) 'Ethnicity, health and health care in the UK', in W. Ahmad, A. Darr and L. Jones, *Health matters*, London: Allen and Unwin.

31   Swain, J., Finkelstein, V., French, S. and Oliver, M. (eds) (1993) *Disabling barriers enabling environments*, London: Sage Publications.

32   Vernon, A. (2002) *Users' views of community care services for disabled people*, York: Joseph Rowntree Foundation.

33   King's Fund (2001) *Future imperfect: Report of the King's Fund Care and Support Inquiry*, London: King's Fund.

34   Social Services Inspectorate (1999) *They look after their own, don't they?, Inspection of community care services for black and minority ethnic people*, London: DH/SSI.

35   Welsh Assembly Government (2002a) *National service framework for working age adults*, Cardiff: WAG.

36   British Medical Association (1995) *Taking care of carers*, London: BMA.

37   Henwood, M. (1998) *Ignored and invisible? Carers' experiences of the NHS*, London: Carers National Association.

38   Hirst, M. (2003) 'Caring-related inequalities in psychological distress in Britain during the 1990s', *Journal of Public Health Medicine*, vol 25, no 4, pp 336-343.

39   Liston, R., Mann, L. and Bannerjee, M. (1995) 'Studies in informal carers of hospitalised elderly patients', *Journal of the Royal College of Physicians*, vol 29.

40   National Assembly of Wales (2000) *Caring about carers: A strategy for carers in Wales*, Cardiff: NAW.

41   Princess Royal Trust (2003) *Primary carers – Identifying and providing support to carers in primary care*, London: PRT.

42   Age Concern (2001) *Opening doors: Working with older lesbians and gay men*, London: Age Concern.

43   Alzheimer's Society Lesbian and Gay Carers Network (2002) *The gay and lesbian carers network – The first two years*, London: Alzheimer's Society.

44   Carers UK (2003) *Missed opportunities: The impact of carers' new rights*, London: Carers UK.

45   Allen, I. and Perkins, E. (1995) *The future of family care for older people*, London: HMSO.

46   Bauld, L., Chesterman, J., Davies, B., Judge, K. and Mangalore, R. (2000) *Caring for older people: An assessment of community care in the 1990s*, Aldershot: Ashgate.

47   Drewett, A., Oldsen, R. and Parker, G. (1994) *Community care and informal carers: Report of the Social Services Inspectorate*, London: SSI.

48   Milne, A. and Hatzidimitriadou, E. (2002) 'The "Caring in later life" report: A secondary analysis of the 1995 General Household Survey', in *Quality in Ageing: Policy, Practice and Research*, vol 3, no 3, pp 315-322.

49	Parker, G. (1998) 'Trends in caring 1985-95', *General Household Survey: Informal carers*, London: Office for National Statistics.

50	Pickard, L. (1999) 'Policy options for informal carers of older people', *With respect to old age: Royal commission report on long-term care*, London: TSO.

51	Audit Commission (2004) *Support for carers of older people: Independence and wellbeing*, London: Audit Commission.

52	Briggs, K. and Ashkam, J. (1999) *The needs of people with dementia and those who care for them*, London: Alzheimer's Society.

53	Moriarty, J. and Webb, S. (2000) *Part of their lives: Community care for older people with dementia*, Bristol: The Policy Press.

54	Walker, A. and Walker, C. (1998) *Uncertain futures: People with learning difficulties and their ageing family carers*, York/Brighton: Joseph Rowntree Foundation/Pavilion.

55	Arber, S. and Ginn, J. (1990) 'The meaning of informal care: Gender and the contribution of older people', *Ageing and Society*, vol 10, no 4, pp 429-454.

56	Dalley, G. (1988) *Ideologies of caring: Rethinking community and collectivism*, London: Macmillan.

57	Finch, J. and Groves, D. (1983) *A labour of love: Women, work and caring*, London: Routledge.

58	Ungerson, C. (1987) *Policy is personal: Sex, gender and informal care*, London: Tavistock.

59	Bornat, J., Johnson, J., Pereira, C., Pilgrim, D. and Williams, F. (eds) (1997) *Community care: A reader*, London: Macmillan.

60	McLaughlin, E. and Ritchie, J. (1994) 'Legacies of caring: The experiences and circumstances of ex-carers', *Health and Social Care in the Community*, vol 7, pp 241-253.

61	Morris, J. (1993) *Independent lives: Community care and disabled people*, Basingstoke: Macmillan.

62	Arksey, H., Hepworth, D. and Qureshi, H. (2000) *Carers' needs and the Carers' Act: An evaluation of the process and outcomes of assessment*, York: Social Policy Research Unit.

63	Carers National Association (1997) *Still battling: The Carers Act one year on*, London: Carers National Association.

64	Davis, A., Ellis, K. and Rummery, K. (1997) *Access to assessment: Perspectives of practitioners, disabled people and carers*, Bristol: The Policy Press.

65 Kersten, P. (2001) 'Needs of carers of severely disabled people: Are they identified and adequately met?', *Health and Social Care in the Community*, vol 5, no 4, pp 235-243.

66 Preston-Shoot, M. (2003) 'Only connect: Client, carer and professional perspectives on community care assessment processes', *Research, Policy and Planning*, vol 21, no 3, pp 23-35.

67 Rummery, K., Ellis, K. and Davis, A. (1999) 'Negotiating access to community care assessments: Perspectives of front-line workers, people with disability and carers', *Health and Social Care in the Community*, vol 7, no 4, pp 296-300.

68 Seddon, D. and Robinson, C. (2001) 'Carers of older people with dementia: Assessment and the Carers Act', *Health and Social Care in the Community*, vol 9, no 3, pp 151-158.

69 Williams, V. (1999) 'In their own right: The support needs of family carers of people with learning difficulties', *Mental Health Care*, vol 3, no 3.

70 Manthorpe, J. (2001) 'Caring at a distance: Learning and practice Issues', *Social Work Education*, vol 20, no 5, pp 593-602.

71 Mitchell, M. (2003) 'Impact of discharge from day surgery on patients and carers', *British Journal of Nursing*, vol 12, no 7, pp 402-408.

72 Carers National Association (2001) *You can take him home now: Carers' experience of hospital discharge*, London: Carers National Association.

73 Carers UK (2005) *Back me up: Planning for emergencies – Carers UK practice briefing*, London: Carers UK.

74 Barnes, M. and Wistow, G. (1992) *Coming out of the wilderness? Carers' views of their consultations and outcomes*, Leeds: Nuffield Institute.

75 Twigg, J. and Atkin, K. (1994) *Carers perceived: Policy and practice in informal care*, Buckingham: Open University Press.

76 Age Concern (1993) *Recognising our voices*, London: Age Concern.

77 Barnes, C. (1991) *Disabled people in Britain and discrimination: A case for anti-discrimination legislation*, London: Hurst Calgary.

78 Barnes, M. (1997) *Care, communities and citizens*, London: Longman.

79 Beresford, P. (1994) *Changing the culture: Involving service users in social work education*, London: Central Council for Education and Training in Social Work.

80 Campbell, J. and Oliver, M. (1996) *Disability politics: Understanding our past, changing our future*, London: Routledge.

81 Goss, S. and Miller, C. (1995) *From margin to mainstream*, York: Joseph Rowntree Foundation.

82 Peck, E. and Barker, I. (1997) 'Users as partners in mental health – ten years of experience', *Journal of Interprofessional Care*, vol 11, pp 269-277.

83 *Carers (Recognition and Services) Act 1995*, London: HMSO.

84 Department of Health (1999) *Caring for carers*, London: TSO.

85 *Carers and Disabled Children Act 2000*, London: TSO.

86 *Community Care (Delayed Discharges, etc) Act 2003*, London: TSO.

87 *Carers (Equal Opportunities) Act 2004*, London: TSO.

88 *Community Care (Direct Payments) Act 1996*, London: TSO.

89 Department of Health (1999) *National service framework for mental health*, London: DH.

90 Department of Health (2001a) *Valuing people: A new strategy for learning disability for the 21st century*, London: HMSO.

91 Princess Royal Trust (2002) *'Carers speak out' project: Report on the main findings and recommendations*, London: PRT.

92 Rethink (2003) *Who cares? The experiences of mental health carers accessing services and information*, London: Rethink.

93 Princess Royal Trust (2004) *Carers' health survey: Main findings*, London: PRT.

94 Department of Health (2001) *Carers and Disabled Children Act: Carers and people with parental responsibility for disabled children – Practice guidance*, London: DH.

95 Stephen Ladyman MP (2005) *Carers and employment: Inclusion and support for carers*, London: DH (available at: www.dh.gov.uk/NewsHome/Speechs/SpeechesList/SpeechesArticle/fs/en).

96 Department of Health (2005) *Beacon status scheme 2005, round 6: Supporting carers* (guidance pack), London: DH.

97 Banks, P. and Cheeseman, C. (1999) *Taking action to support carers: A carers' impact guide for commissioners and managers*, London: King's Fund.

98 Department of Health/Social Services Inspectorate (2002) *Modernising services to transform care: Inspection of how councils are managing the modernisation agenda in social care*, London: SSI.

99   Association of Directors of Social Services (2002) 'Carers would directly benefit from additional resources – ADSS' (ADSS press release), 25 April.

100 Exworthy, M. and Halford, S. (1999) *Professionals and managerialism in the new public sector*, Buckingham: Open University Press.

101 Bland, R. (ed) (1996) *Developing services for older people and their families*, London: Jessica Kingsley Publishing.

102 Nolan, M., Grant, G. and Keady, J. (1998) *Assessing the needs of family carers: A guide for practitioners*, Brighton: Pavilion.

103 Carers UK (2002) *Without us? Calculating the value of carers' support*, London: Carers UK.

104 Corti, L,. Laurie, H. and Dex, S. (1994) *Caring and employment*, Colchester: ESRC Research Centre on Micro-social Change/University of Essex/Department of Employment.

105 Department for Education and Employment (2000) *Work–life balance: Changing patterns in a changing world*, London: DfEE.

106 Department of Trade and Industry (1998) *Fairness at Work*, London: DTI.

107 Department of the Environment, Transport and the Regions (1998) *Modern local government – In touch with the people*, London: TSO.

108 European Foundation for the Improvement of Living and Working Conditions (1996) *Working and caring: Developments at the workplace for family carers of older and disabled people*, Dublin: EFILWC.

109 Institute for Personnel Management (1990) *Work and the family: Carer-friendly employment practice*, London: IPM.

110 Phillips, J. (ed.) (1995) *Working carers*, Aldershot: Avebury.

111 *Employment Relations Act 1999*, London: TSO.

112 *Carers and Direct Payments Act (Northern Ireland) 2002*, London: TSO.

113 Department of Health, Social Services and Public Safety (Northern Ireland) and Carers Northern Ireland (2002) *Valuing carers: Proposals for a strategy for carers in Northern Ireland*, Belfast: DHSSPS.

114 Department of Health, Social Services and Public Safety (2005) *Standards to improve quality in health and social care*, Belfast: DHSSPS.

115 Northern Ireland Social Services Inspectorate (2005) *Final draft standards for inspection of social care support services for carers of older people: Key standards and criteria*, Belfast: SSI.

116 Halliday, B. and Dixon, P. (1996) 'Perceptions of care management within a Northern Ireland health and social services board', *Elders: The Journal of Care and Practice*, vol 5, no 3, pp 20-28.

117 Welsh Assembly Government (2000a) *Caring about carers: Strategy Report*, Cardiff: WAG.

118 Welsh Assembly Government (2000b) *Carers' strategy implementation plan,* Cardiff: WAG.

119 Welsh Assembly Government (2001) *Equity, empowerment, effectiveness and efficiency: Adult mental health strategy*, Cardiff: WAG/AMHS.

120 All Wales Ethnic Minority Asssociation– (2002) *Challenging the myth: Access issues for BME carers in Wales*, Cardiff: AWEMA.

121 Welsh Assembly Government/Adult Mental Health Services (2004) *Stronger in partnership: Involving users and carers in the design, planning, delivery and evaluation of mental health services in Wales – Policy implementation guide*, Cardiff: WAG.

122 Department of Health (2000a) *The NHS plan: A plan for investment, a plan for reform*, London: DH.

123 Department of Health (2000b) *A quality strategy for social care*, London: DH.

124 Department of Health (2001c) *Better care, higher standards: Guidance for 2001/2*, London: DH.

125 Pitkeathly, J. (1996) *Carers – Research matters*, London: Carers National Association.

126 Oliver, M. and Sapey, B. (1999) *Social work with disabled people*, London: Jessica Kingsley Publishing.

127 Hudson, B. (2000) *The changing role of social care*, London: Jessica Kingsley Publishing.

128 Means, R. and Smith, R. (2003) *Community care, policy and practice*, Basingstoke: Macmillan.

129 Carr, S. (2004) *Has service user participation made a difference to social care services?*, SCIE Position Paper 3, London: SCIE.

130 Rickford, J. (2000) 'Value judgements', *Community Care*, no 1348, pp 20-22.

131 Barker, R. and Roberts, H. (1993) 'The uses of the concept of power', in D. Morgan and L. Stanley (eds) *Debates in sociology*, Manchester: Manchester University Press.

132 Dominelli, L. (2002) *Anti-oppressive social work and practice*, London: Routledge.

133 Pickard, L., Wittenberg, R., Comas-Herrera, A., Davies, B. and Darton, R. (2000) 'Relying on informal care in the new century? Informal care for elderly people in England to 2031', *Ageing and Society*, vol 20, pp 747-772.

134 Clarke, M. and Stewart, J. (1992) 'Empowerment: A theme for the 1990s', *Local Government Studies*, vol 18, no 2, pp 18-26.

135 Parsloe, P. and Stevenson, O. (1996) *Community care and empowerment*, York: Joseph Rowntree Foundation.

136 Beresford, P. and Croft, S. (1993) *Citizen involvement: A practical guide for change*, Basingstoke: Macmillan.

137 Barnes, C., Mercer, G. and Shakespeare, T. (1999) *Exploring disability: A sociological introduction*, Cambridge: Polity Press.

138 Braye, S. and Preston-Shoot, M. (1995) *Empowering practice in social care*, Buckingham: Open University Press.

139 Croft, S. and Beresford, P. (1995) 'Whose empowerment? Equalising the competing discourses in community care', in R. Jack (ed) *Empowerment in community care*, London: Chapman.

140 Hugman, R. (1998) *Social work and social value: The role of caring professions*, Basingstoke: Longman.

141 Swain, J., French, S., Barnes, C. and Thomas, C. (eds) (2004) *Disabling barriers – Enabling environments*, London: Sage Publications.

142 Borsay, A. (2004) *Disability and policy in Britain since 1750*, London: Palgrave Macmillan.

143 Finkelstein, V. and Stuart, O. (1996) 'Developing new services', in G. Hales (ed) *Beyond disability – Towards an enabling society*, London: Sage Publications.

144 Hughes, G. (1998) 'A suitable case for treatment?', in E. Saraga (ed) *Embodying the social: Constructions of disability*, London: Routledge.

145 Alzheimer's Society (2003) *Choices in care*, London: Alzheimer's Society.

146 Ryan, T. and Bamber, C. (2002) 'A survey of policy and practice on expenses and other payments to mental health service users and carers participating in service delivery', *Journal of Mental Health*, vol 11, no 6, pp 635-644.

147 Social Services Inspectorate (1998) *A matter of chance for carers? Inspection of local authority support for carers*, London: DH.

148 Afiya Trust (2001) *We care too – A good practice guide for people working with black carers*, London: Afiya Trust.

149 National Black Carers' Workers Network (2000) *Black carers manifesto*, London: NBCWN.

150 Williams, V. and Robinson, C. (2000) *In their own right: The Carers' Act and carers of people with learning difficulties*, Bristol: The Policy Press.

151 Edwards, A. (2002) 'What is "knowledge" in social care?', *MCC Building Knowledge for Integrated Care*, vol 10, no 1, pp 13-16.

152 Arnstein, S. (1969) 'A ladder of citizen', *Journal of the American Institute of Planners*, vol 35, no 4, pp 216-224.

153 Casey, A. (1995) 'Partnership nursing: Influences on involvement of informal carers', *Journal of Advanced Nursing*, vol 22, no 6, pp 1058-1062.

154 Audit Commission (1999) *Listen up: Effective community consultation*, London: Audit Commission.

155 Robinson, C. and Williams, V. (2002) 'Carers of people with learning disabilities, and their experience of the 1995 Carers Act', *British Journal of Social Work*, vol 32, no 2, pp 169-183.

156 Williams, V. and Robinson, C. (2000) *In their own right: The Carers Act and carers of people with learning disabilities*, Bristol: The Policy Press.

157 Williams, V. (1999) 'In their own right: The support needs of family carers of people with learning difficulties', *Mental Health Care*, vol 3, no 3, pp 94-95.

158 Pickard, L. (2001) 'Carer break or carer-blind? Policies for informal carers in the UK', *Social Policy and Administration*, vol 35, no 4, pp 441-458.

159 Walker, E. and Dewar, B. (2001) 'How do we facilitate carers' involvement in decision-making?', *Journal of Advanced Nursing*, vol 34, no 3, pp 329-337.

160 Clegg, A. (2003) 'Older South Asian patient and carer perceptions of culturally sensitive care in a community hospital setting', *Journal of Clinical Nursing*, vol 12, no 2, pp 283-290.

161 Wenger, G., Scott, A. and Seddon, D. (2002) 'The experience of caring for older people with dementia in a rural area: Using services', *Ageing and Mental Health*, vol 6, no 1, pp 30-38.

162 McGarry, J. and Arthur, A. (2001) 'Informal caring in late life: A qualitative study of the experiences of older carers', *Journal of Advanced Nursing*, vol 33, no 2, pp 182-189.

163 Simpson, E. and House, A. (2003) 'User and carer involvement in mental health services: From rhetoric to science', *British Journal of Psychiatry*, vol 183, pp 89-91.

164 McKeown, L., Porter-Armstrong, A. and Baxter, G. (2003) 'The needs and experiences of caregivers of individuals with multiple sclerosis: A systemic review', *Clinical Rehabilitation*, vol 17, no 3, pp 234-248.

165 Chambers, M. and Connor, S.L. (2002) 'User-friendly technology to help family carers cope', *Journal of Advanced Nursing*, vol 40, no 5, pp 568-577.

166 Dewar, B., Tocher, R. and Watson, W. (2003) 'Enhancing partnerships with relatives in care settings', *Nursing Standard*, vol 17, no 40, pp 33-39.

167 Last, A. (2003) 'User involvement: Pick and choose', *Health Service Journal*, vol 113, no 5852, pp 28-29.

168 Scott, G., Whyler, N. and Grant, G. (2001) 'A study of family carers of people with a life-threatening illness 1: The carers' needs analysis', *International Journal of Palliative Nursing*, vol 7, no 6, pp 290-291.

169 Clarke, N. (2001) 'Training as a vehicle to empower carers in the community: More than a question of information sharing', *Health and Social Care in the Community*, vol 9, no 2, pp 79-88.

170 Simpson, R. (1997) 'Carers as equal partners in care planning', *Journal of Psychiatric Mental Health Nursing*, vol 4, no 5, pp 345-354.

171 Dening, T. and Lawton, C. (1998) 'The role of carers in evaluating mental health services for older people', *International Journal of Geriatric Psychiatry*, vol 13, no 12, pp 863-870.

172 Woods, R., Wills, W., Higginson, I., Hobbins, J. and Whitby, M. (2003) 'Support in the community for people with dementia and their carers: A comparative outcome study of specialist mental health service interventions', *International Journal of Geriatric Psychiatry*, vol 18, no 4, pp 298-307.

173 Hardy, B., Young, R. and Wistow, G. (1999) 'Dimensions of choice in the assessment and care management process: The views of older people, carers and care managers', *Health and Social Care in the Community*, vol 7, no 6, pp 483-491.

174 Nicholas, E. (2003) 'An outcome focus in carer assessment and review: Value and challenge', *British Journal of Social Work*, vol 33, no 1, pp 31-48.

175 Henderson, J. (2001) '"He's not my carer – he's my husband": Personal and policy constructions of care in mental health', *Journal of Social Work Practice*, vol 15, no 2, pp 149-160.

176 Mitchell, F. (1996) 'Carer support groups', *Practice*, vol 8, no 4, pp 53-59.

177 Mitchell, F. (1996) 'Carer support groups: The effects of organisational factors on the character of the groups', *Health and Social Care in the Community*, vol 4, no 2, pp 113-121.

178 Gillies, B. (2000) 'Acting up: Role ambiguity and the legal recognition of carers', *Ageing and Society*, vol 20, pp 429-444.

179 Arksey, H., Hepworth, D. and Qureshi, H. (2000) *Carers' needs and the Carers Act: An evaluation of the process and outcomes of assessment*, York: Social Policy Research Unit, University of York.

180 Arksey, H. (2002) 'Rationed care: Assessing the support needs of informal carers in English social services authorities', *Journal of Social Policy*, vol 31, no 1, pp 81-101.

181 Nolan, M. (2001) 'Working with family carers: Towards a partnership approach', *Reviews in Clinical Gerontology,* vol 11, pp 91-97.

182 Henderson, J. and Forbat, L. (2002) 'Relationship-based social policy: Personal and policy constructions of "care",' *Critical Social Policy*, vol 22, no 4, pp 665-683.

183 Nichol, M., Ashworth, M., McNally, L. and Newman, S. (2002) 'Satisfaction with respite care: A pilot study', *Health and Social Care in the Community*, vol 10, no 6, pp 479-484.

184 Olsen, R., Parker, G. and Drewett, A. (1997) 'Carers and the missing link: Changing professional attitudes', *Health and Social Care in the Community*, vol 5, no 2, pp 116-123.

185 Rhodes, P. and Shaw, S. (1999) 'Informal care and terminal illness', *Health and Social Care in the Community*, vol 7, no 1, pp 39-50.

186 Simon, C., Little, P., Birtwistle, J. and Kendrick, T. (2003) 'A questionnaire to measure satisfaction with community services for informal carers of stroke patients: Construction and initial piloting', *Health and Social Care in the Community*, vol 11, no 2, pp 129-137.

187 Smith, F., Francis, S.-A., Gray, N., Denham, M. and Graffy, J. (2003) 'A multi-centre survey among informal carers who manage medication for older care recipients: Problems experienced and development of services', *Health and Social Care in the Community*, vol 11, no 2, pp 138-145.

188 Baker, C., Edwards, P. and Packer, T. (2003) 'Crucial impact of the world surrounding dementia care', *Journal of Dementia Care*, vol 11, no 3, pp 16-18.

189 Nolan, M., Ingram, P. and Watson, R. (2002) 'Working with family carers of people with dementia: "Negotiated" coping as an essential outcome', *Dementia: The Journal of Social Research and Practice*, vol 1, no 1, pp 75-93.

190 Barr, A., Stenhouse, C. and Henderson, P. (2001) *Caring communities: A challenge for social exclusion*. York: York Publishing Services/Joseph Rowntree Foundation.

191 Finch, J. (1999) 'Involving users and carers in developing standards for mental health services for older people', *Managing Community Care*, vol 7, no 6, pp 25-29.

192 Middleton, T. (2001) 'Mental health services for older people: Towards an integrated approach', *Mental Health Review*, vol 6, no 2, pp 22-24.

193 Heaton, J., Arksey, H. and Sloper, P. (1999) 'Carers' experiences of hospital discharge and continuing care in the community', *Health and Social Care in the Community*, vol 7, no 2, pp 91-99.

194 Arksey, H., Heaton, J. and Sloper, P. (1997) *Coming home: Carers' views on hospital discharge arrangements for younger disabled people*, York: Social Policy Research Unit, University of York.

195 Heron, C. (1998) *Working with carers*, London: Jessica Kingsley Publishing.

196 Beck, R. and Minghella, E. (1998) 'Home alone', *Health Service Journal*, 4 June, pp 30-31.

197 Carpenter, J. and Sbaraini, S. (1997) *Choice, information and dignity: Involving users and carers in care management in mental health*, Bristol: The Policy Press.

198 Arksey, H., Jackson, K., Croucher, K., Weatherly, H., Golder, S., Hare, P., Newbronner, E. and Baldwin, S. (2004) *Review of respite services and short-term breaks for carers for people with dementia*, York: Social Policy Research Unit, University of York.

199 Ward, C. (2001) *Family matters: Counting families in*, London: D.

200 Hepworth, D. (2002) *Improving assessment and support for South Asian carers*, York: Sir Halley Stewart Trust/Social Policy Research Unit, University of York.

201 Heenan, D. (2000) 'Informal care in farming families in Northern Ireland: Some considerations for social work', *British Journal of Social Work*, vol 30, pp 855-866.

202 Arksey, H., Jackson, K., Wallace, A., Baldwin, S., Golder, S., Newbonner, E. and Hare, P. (2003) *Access to health care for carers: Barriers and interventions – Report for the National Coordinating Centre for NHS Delivery and Organisation RandD (NCCSDO)*, York: Social Policy Research Unit, University of York.

203 Manthorpe, J. (2003) 'Nearest and dearest? The neglect of lesbians in caring relationships', *British Journal of Social Work*, vol 33, no 6, pp 753-768.

204 Ashworth, M. and Baker, A. (2000) '"Time and space": Carers' views about respite care', *Health and Social Care in the Community*, vol 8, no 1, pp 50-56.

205 Newbronner, E. and Hare, P. (2002) *Services to support carers of people with mental health problems: Consultation report for the National Co-ordinating Centre for NHS Service Delivery and Organisation RandD (NCCSDO)*, York: Social Policy Research Unit, University of York.

206 Warner, L. and Wexler, S. (1998) *Eight hours a day and taken for granted: You just get on with it, don't you?*, London: Princess Royal Trust for Carers.

207 Keeley, B. and Clarke, M. (2002) *Carers speak out*, London: PRT.

208 Macgregor, M. and Hill, M. (2003) *Missed opportunities: The impact of new rights for carers*, London: Carers UK.

209 Powell, E. (2002) *We care too: A good practice guide for people working with black carers*, London: Afiya Trust/National Black Carers Workers Network.

210 Princess Royal Trust (2003) *Focus on carers and the NHS: Identifying and supporting hidden carers - Good practice guide*, London: PRT.

211 Social Services Inspectorate (1999) *They look after their own, don't they? Inspection of community care services for black and ethnic minority older people*, London: DH/SSI.

212 Royal College of Nursing/Unison (2004) *Not 'just' a friend: Best practice on health care guidance for lesbian, gay and bisexual service users and their families*, London: Royal College of Nursing.

213 Manthorpe, J., Alaszewski, A., Gates, B., Ayer, S. and Motherby, A. (2003) 'Learning disability nursing: User and carer perceptions', *Journal of Learning Disabilities* vol 7, no 2, pp 119-135.

214 Simpson, A. (1999) 'Creating alliances: The views of users and carers on the education and training needs of community mental health nurses', *Journal of Psychiatric and Mental Health Nursing*, vol 6, no 5, pp 347-356.

215 Manthorpe, J. (2000) 'Developing carers' contributions to social work training', *Social Work Education*, vol 19, no 1, pp 19-27.

216 Molyneux, J. and Irvine, J. (2004) 'Service user and carer involvement in social work training: A long and winding road?', *Social Work Education*, vol 23, no 4, pp 293-308.

217 Turner, P., Sheldon, F., Coles, C., Mountford, B., Hillier, R., Radawy, P. and Wee, B. (2000) 'Listening to and learning from the family carer's story: An innovative approach in interprofessional education', *Journal of Interprofessional Care*, vol 14, no 4, pp 387-395.

218 Lister, S., Mitchell, W., Sloper, W. and Roberts, K. (2003) 'Participation and partnerships in research: Listening to the ideas and experiences of a parent-carer', *International Journal of Social Research Methodology*, vol 6, no 2, pp 159-165.

219 Hanson, E., Tetley, J. and Clarke, A. (1999) 'A multimedia intervention to support family caregivers', *Gerontologist*, vol 39, no 6, pp 736-741.

220 Hanson, E. and Clarke, A. (2000) 'The role of telematics in assisting family carers and frail people at home', *Health and Social Care in the Community*, vol 8, no 2, pp 129-137.

221 Lloyd, M. and Carson, A. (2005) 'Culture shift: Carer empowerment and cooperative inquiry', *Journal of Psychiatric and Mental Health Nursing*, vol 12, no 2, pp 187-191.

222 Milne, A. (2004) 'Culture and care in dementia', *Updates: Research and policy briefings from the Mental Health Foundation*, vol 5, no 5.

223 Preston-Shoot, M. (2003) 'Only connect: Client, carer and professional perspectives on community care assessment processes', *Research, Policy and Planning*, vol 21, no 3, pp 23-35.

224 Simon, C., Kumar, S. and Kendrick, T. (2002) 'Who cares for the carers? The district nurse perspective', *Family Practice*, vol 19, no 1, pp 29-35.

225 Noble, D. and Bateman, N. (1995) *Respite – The way forward in Kent*, Canterbury: Kent Action for Respite Choice/Kent Social Services/East Kent Health Authority.

226 Qureshi, H., Bamford, C., Nicholas, E., Patmore, C. and Harris, J. (2000) *Implementing an outcomes approach to carer assessment and review: Social Policy Research Unit report for the Department of Health*, York: Social Policy Research Unit.

227 Lelliott, P., Beevor, A., Hogman, G., Hyslop, J., Lathlean, J. and Ward, M. (2003) 'Carers' and users' expectations of services – carer version (cues-c): A new instrument to support the assessment of carers of people with severe mental illness', *Journal of Mental Health*, vol 12, no 2, pp143-152.

228 Seddon, D. and Robinson, C. (2004) 'Supporting carers in paid work', *Working with Older People*, vol 8, no 2, pp 13-18.

229 Seddon, D. (1999) 'Negotiating caregiving and employment', in S. Cox and J. Keady (eds) *Younger people with dementia: Planning, practice and development*, London: Jessica Kingsley Publishing.

230 Turner, S. and Street, H. (1999) 'Assessing carers training needs: A pilot enquiry', *Aging and Mental Health*, vol 3, no 2, pp 173-178.

231 Pickard, S., Jacobs, S. and Kirk, S. (2003) 'Challenging professional roles: Lay carers' involvement in health care in the community', *Social Policy and Administration*, vol 37, no 1, pp 82-96.

232 Manthorpe, J. and Twigg, J. (1995) 'Carers and care management', *Baseline*, vol 59, pp 4-8.

233 Rethink (2003) *Who cares? The experiences of mental health carers accessing services and information*, London: Rethink.

234 Harding, R. and Higginson, I. (2003) 'What is the best way to help caregivers in cancer and palliative care? A systematic literature review of interventions and their effectiveness', *Palliative Medicine*, vol 17, no 17, pp 63-74.

235 Social Services Inspectorate (2002) *Modernising services to transform care: Inspection of how councils are managing the modernisation agenda in social care*, London: SSI/DH.

236 Yeandle, S., Crompton, R., Wigfield, A. and Dennet, J. (2002) *Employed carers and family friendly policies*, Bristol: The Policy Press.

237 Jarvis, A. and McIntosh, G. (2004) 'The recognition and support of carers', *Professional Nurse*, vol 20, no 4, pp 24-26.

238 Dewar, B., Goulbourne, A., Irvine, L. and Riddell, H. (2002) 'The carer's role in planning care for people with dementia', *Professional Nurse*, vol 17, no 5, pp 318-321.

239 Goulbourne, A., Dewar, B., Irvine, L. and Riddell, H. (2001) *A project to validate guidelines which seek to involve lay carers of people with dementia in carer planning processes: Final report*, Edinburgh: Queen Margaret University College.

240 Carers National Association (2001) *You can take him home now: Carers' experiences of hospital discharge*, London: Carers National Association.

241 Carers UK (2005) *Back me up: Supporting carers when they need it most*, London: Carers UK.

242 Foundation for People with Learning Disabilities (2003) *Planning for tomorrow*, London: FPLD.

243 Rogers, H. (1996) 'Breaking the ice: Developing strategies for collaborative working with carers of older people with mental health problems', in H. Kemshall and R. Littlewood (eds) (2000) *User involvement and participation in social care*, London: Jessica Kingsley Publishing.

244 Katbamna, S., Ahmad, W., Bhaktar, P., Baker, R. and Parker, G. 2004) 'Do they look after their own? Informal support in South Asian families', *Health and Social Care in the Community*, vol 12, no 5, pp 398-406.

245 Took, M. (1999) 'Involving service users and carers', *Journal of Psychiatric and Mental Health Nursing*, vol 6, no 6, pp 485-487.

246 Forbat, L. and Nar, S. (2003) 'Dementia's cultural challenge', *Community Care*, vol 1491, pp 38-39.

247 Forbat, L. (2003) 'Concepts and understandings of dementia by gatekeepers of minority ethnic service users', *British Journal of Health Psychology*, vol 8, no 3, pp 645-655.

248 Department of Health (2002) *Developing services for carers and families of people with mental illness*, London: DH.

Appendix A: Involving carers

August 2004
Aim Early meeting with carers to discuss the remit and focus of the paper and its constituent research.
Outcome Carers influenced definitions of carers and emphasised the significance of care settings beyond the home (for example, liaising with acute healthcare, etc).

September 2004
Aim Discuss carer diversity and inclusivity – for example, the need to involve lesbian and gay carers, carers of those involved with substance misuse and lifetime carers.
Outcome The remit of the research was widened and the research team's breadth of carer awareness enhanced.

October 2004
Aim 1 Explore with carers the design of the survey questionnaire and the best way to garner voluntary sector, carers' organisations' and carer responses.
Aim 2 Review the draft questionnaire and aid piloting.
Outcome An example of the input of carers was the rewording of many of the questions to make them more carer-friendly. This helped maximise valid contacts with carers' organisations and carers. It allowed questions to be tested and reviewed in a way that made the questionnaire best able to evince wider carer responses.

November 2004
Aim 1 Advise on how best to contact carers while approval from the ADSS was awaited.
Aim 2 Advise and pilot draft interview protocols.
Outcome Carers suggested that we access carers via PRT carers' centre networks, which would help the project keep to schedule while not breaking ADSS protocols. Carers helped establish what would and would not work in the interview schedules.

December/January 2004/05
Aim 1 Carers asked to scrutinise the first data responses from the survey of statutory and voluntary agencies.
Aim 2 Carers agreed that interview matching would be valuable and volunteers came forward for carer interviews. Carers suggested training would be helpful.
Outcome Carers aided the interpretation of Stage 1 (survey) data and agreed with the research how best to import these into Stage 2 for further examination. Carers successfully undertook interviews in January 2005.

January/February 2005
Aim Carers asked to triangulate the Stage 1 and 2 data, in partnership with the research team, and to make suggestions as to the interpretation of some raw research findings. Also asked to comment on how the draft Position Paper should be presented.
Outcome Carers provided a unique perspective on how wider carer constituencies might view the final report. Comments on issues that required further analysis were made, which highlighted issues for the writing-up process.

informants and professionals. Many carers were found to have continued barriers to accessing short breaks.

Arnstein, S. (1969) 'A ladder of citizen', *Journal of the American Institute of Planners,* **vol 35, no 4, pp 216-224.**
Arnstein's notion of a ladder of participation is a key conceptual and typological contribution to our understanding of participation and the many gradations of carer and user involvement. This article has served as a key direction marker for much service thinking and best practice in service and carer participation. This conceptual framework and its higher order concepts of participation comes closest to an industry standard benchmark in carer inclusive working.

Ashworth, M. and Baker, A. (2000) '"Time and space": Carers' views about respite care', *Health and Social Care in the Community,* **vol 8, no 1, pp 50-56.**
A qualitative study of carer's views of respite services. Carers (*n*=23) were interviewed using a semi-structured schedule. Themes were identified. Carers made sense of how respite reduces the costs of caring (physical exhaustion, feelings of despair, lack of recognition and financial loss). While agreeing that it is clearly beneficial in establishing a sense of normality and freedom, carers were concerned that respite care use might be viewed as carer failure.

Audit Commission (1999) *Listen up: Effective community consultation,* **London: Audit Commission.**
This policy-driven report uses surprisingly direct language to get across its message that service providers and professionals have to 'listen up' if more enabling partnership working is to be established.

Audit Commission (2004) *Support for carers of older people: Independence and wellbeing,* **London: Audit Commission.**
This multimethod study formed part of a suite of studies on older people, independence and well-being. Alongside a major consultation exercise with key carer stakeholders, the study looked at support and services for older people in six diverse areas of England (county council, unitary authority, inner and outer London boroughs). The questionnaires were sent to 200 'known carers' in each of the six designated areas and approximately 480 of them responded (this response rate – 40% – is higher than for most larger surveys). Contacts were gleaned from council and voluntary-sector (carers') organisation databases. Interviews were also held with a range of care stakeholders in each area – from lead officers through social work assistants in SSDs and care leads in PCTs to senior voluntary sector staff. Focus groups were held with an unspecified number of carers. Case files of recent care assessments were also examined.

Baker, C., Edwards, P. and Packer, T. (2003) 'Crucial impact of the world surrounding dementia care', *Journal of Dementia Care,* **vol 11, no 3, pp 16-18.**
This technical article details pilot attempts to operationalise carer involvement protocols in person-centred care. The work is part of the DH 'Essence of Care' and aims to add an operationalised and empowering carer involvement strand to this programme. Typologies of support (akin to those developed by Arnstein, Goss and others) provide guidance on benchmarking good practice. It is unclear how carers have been involved (if at all) in the formulation of the protocols.

Barr, A., Stenhouse, C. and Henderson, P. (2001) *Caring communities: A challenge for social exclusion*, **York: York Publishing Services/Joseph Rowntree Foundation.**
This action research project had a diverse constituency, and was based on an evaluation of the impact of social inclusion policy in four Scottish localities. A decision was made to include this study in the present Position Paper as it has wider implications and a more encompassing remit, plus it contains an evaluation of policy impact on Asian carers, a subject that is little understood at grassroots level. Alongside planned demonstration projects in each locality, training, consultancy and evaluation were all offered. The degree of impact on policy and practice was the key focus of the research. One project looked at the participation of Asian carers in inner-city Glasgow and the potential for social work interventions to empower carers. Multiple methods were used to provide evidence of impact: two questionnaires (completion method unstated) to establish issues and clarify project goals, with one completed at the start of project and one at the end; participant observation; documentary records; focus groups; and key informant interviews. However, in the Asian carers project, a case study approach was adopted rather than participant observation.

Beck, R. and Minghella, E. (1998) 'Home alone', *Health Service Journal*, **November, pp 30-31.**
This study looked at the shortfall in current support for family carers of people with severe mental illness, and how carers could be better supported, trained and informed. Carers (n=75) were interviewed with a schedule of both open and closed questions. Carer stress and the need for greater access to services and assessment were noted. Carers requested more involvement in treatment and care and to be in partnership with mental health professionals.

Carers UK (2005) *Back me up: Supporting carers when they need it most*, **London: Carers UK.**
This study of carer emergencies – for example, illness or accident of the primary carer – surveyed 1,207 carers. Although this was a large survey, the findings were analysed and presented as qualitative carer stories. It is unclear which criteria were adopted to select these stories from the main survey sample. The research identified significant gaps between emergency planning needs and service realities. The need to ensure that wider emergency planning takes place and the requirement for regular reviews of these plans are key messages for LAs.

Carpenter, J. and Sbaraini, S. (1997) *Choice, information and dignity: Involving users and carers in care management in mental health*, **Bristol: The Policy Press.**
This was a participatory study of the involvement of users and carers in the CPA with people with severe and long-term mental health difficulties. Can users and carers be fruitfully involved in care planning in this area? The study was designed with the active input of carers and service users, in addition to the contributions of mental health professionals (n=53). Carers and users took part in interviewing and constituted part of the research advisory group. Carers (n=20) and users (n=109) were interviewed for Stage 1 of the study. A further interview to reflect on study impact was undertaken with sub-samples of the Stage 1 cohort (44 users, 8 carers). Care management programme changes were prompted by the study.

Casey, A. (1995) 'Partnership nursing: Influences on involvement of informal carers', *Journal of Advanced Nursing*, **vol 22, no 6, pp 1058-1062.**
This study of 243 patients in two children's hospitals looked at factors influencing partnership nursing with informal carers in a hospital setting. Structured interviews with nursing staff, examination of secondary sources (medical and nursing records) and ward observations of 243 children and their families were undertaken. Variables affecting likely involvement were length of time the child had been in hospital: children with chronic conditions had greater parental involvement. Whether the family spoke English was a statistically significant factor limiting involvement. The article also provides a conceptual reflection on how nurses could more effectively engage parent carers in decision making in a hospital context.

Chamba, R., Waqar, A., Hirst, M., Lawton, D. and Beresford, B. (1999) *On the edge: Minority ethnic families caring for a severely disabled child,* **York/Bristol: Joseph Rowntree Foundation/The Policy Press.**
This national collaborative research looked at the often-ignored needs of black carers of 'severely' disabled children and compared findings on carer provision with a study of white carers. The study took the form of a postal questionnaire despatched to about 600 BME parents caring for severely disabled children. The research tool was modelled on a similar study of white carers of severely disabled children (Beresford, 1995). The Family Fund database was used as the basis of the non-random sampling. BME carers were found to face even greater barriers and disadvantage than the (already disadvantaged) white comparator.

Chambers, M. and Connor, S.L. (2002) 'User-friendly technology to help family carers cope', *Journal of Advanced Nursing*, **vol 40, no 5, pp 568-577.**
This usability trial looked at the potential of ICTs in supporting family carers. The trial was performed in two stages. User trials and evaluation questionnaires were used to refine a multimedia software application that facilitated access to information, advice and psychological support. Second-stage questionnaires evaluated the usability of the modified software application. Although imperfect, the application was seen to offer greater potential for family carer independence. Carers had a central role in refining the software based on personal experience.

Clarke, N. (2001) 'Training as a vehicle to empower carers in the community: More than a question of information sharing', *Health and Social Care in the Community,* **vol 9, no 2, pp 79-88.**
This project aimed to apply a critical framework to carer empowerment by appraising the benefits (if any) of carer empowerment training. The carers (n=18) who agreed to take part in the training reflect, claim the researchers, the national profile of carers by sex, type of carer and length of time spent as a carer. The carers were questioned on their levels of psychological empowerment before and after the training (no control group was noted). No obvious training impact on carer empowerment was noted in the measure of psychological empowerment adopted. The researchers argue for much more research into the empowerment process and caution against simple non-reflexive schemes that assume involvement equals empowerment.

Clegg, A. (2003) 'Older South Asian patient and carer perceptions of culturally sensitive care in a community hospital setting', *Journal of Clinical Nursing*, **vol 12, no 2, pp 283-290.**
This study of four patients and three carers of South Asian origin explored what was meant by 'culturally sensitive' services that took account of carers' and patients' needs and expectations. The study was situated in two community hospitals in nurse-led intermediate settings, in inner-city locations. Grounded (inductive) theory and methods were applied to the oral findings from patients and carers. This approach eschewed the notion that pre-formed deductive reasoning would tell us little about culturally sensitive understandings.

Dening, T. and Lawton, C. (1998) 'The role of carers in evaluating mental health services for older people', *International Journal of Geriatric Psychiatry*, **vol 13, no 12, pp 863-870.**
In this study of carers of older people, many with mental health problems, a literature review and local service evaluation constitute the two key methods. A range of service contexts were explored in the context of the wider literature. This was essentially a clinical reflection that included an appraisal of the authors' own local clinical context in which carers have been involved: in initial consultation over care and clinical issues; in extensive and repeated discussions (method unstated); and by the establishment of a carer liaison group. The article highlights the limited nature of participation, with carers being involved in non-strategic decisions, advising on how rather than if/why – for example, on a hospital closure that may impact carers.

Department of Health (2002) *Developing services for carers and families of people with mental illness*, **London: DH.**
This document, although not based on primary research, is included as it uses a research synthesis approach in a way that brings together best practice examples for supporting carers and families who themselves are supporting relatives with mental illness. This is valuable research for local mental health service providers and in developing and sustaining carer support services. Documentary as well as stakeholder contacts were undertaken in compiling the guidance.

Dewar, B., Tocher, R. and Watson, W. (2003) 'Enhancing partnerships with relatives in care settings', *Nursing Standard*, **vol 17, no 40, pp 33-39.**
This action-oriented research involved data collection on how carer involvement was being handled at ward level. A total of 20 carers and 18 qualified and assistant nursing staff were interviewed about it. The data obtained in this way was then fed back to staff to enhance professional practice. Carer involvement priorities were identified and benchmarked against established markers of satisfactory involvement – *see* M. Walker (1999) *Guidelines to facilitate the involvement of lay carers in carer planning of a person with dementia*, Edinburgh: Queen Margaret College, University of Edinburgh.

Dewar, B., Goulbourne, A., Irvine, L. and Riddell, H. (2002) 'The carer's role in planning care for people with dementia', *Professional Nurse*, **vol 17, no 5, pp 318-321.**
This study, by a research team of nursing professionals, evaluated guidance offered to carers of people with dementia on involving those carers in care planning. Nineteen 'lay family carers' of people with dementia agreed to evaluate the guidance with

the aim of commenting on and hopefully enhancing the guidance. They could use either focus groups or written formats to give feedback on the guidance's efficacy and coverage. The research gathered the responses together and presented them to the carers in an iterative process for possible confirmation of the findings. Although they identified ways to improve the guidelines, the carers felt that this alone would not alter their level of influence in care planning and expressed a need for greater involvement in the way that the guidance is applied. A follow-up study is under way to look at the implementation of the suggested changes.

Finch, J. (1999) 'Involving users and carers in developing standards for mental health services for older people', *Managing Community Care*, vol 7, no 6, pp 25-29.
This project sat within the auspices of the Health Advisory Service 2000 Standards Development Programme and had a focus on mental health services for older people. To further the evidence-based evaluation standards, the project involved users and carers to help formulate best practice standards. As well as statutory and voluntary input, users and carers were consulted on the draft standards. Group facilitators met with them to get their comments on tightening the wording and themes of the draft, and a series of more focused meetings followed. Carers were seen to have a crucial role in defining and redefining the standards.

Forbat, L. and Nar, S. (2003) 'Dementia's cultural challenge', *Community Care*, vol 1491, pp 38-39.
Asian and African-Caribbean carers (*n*=12] were researched using interviews about their interaction with formal services. While access to services was facilitated by social workers and Alzheimer's Society staff, culturally sensitive and equitable professional interventions were still more a hope than a reality. The study concludes by asking for the many and varied UK government policy documents to be effected in full.

Foundation for People with Learning Disabilities (2003) *Planning for tomorrow*, London: FPLD.
This is a study of a learning disability partnership board's responses to *Valuing people* and its emphasis on meeting the needs of older family carers of people with learning disabilities. Although not a study of carers *per se*, this is important research in identifying involvement deficits and ideas as to how LDPBs could involve this group more. Questionnaires were despatched to 170 lead officers on LDPBs and 70 completed questionnaires were returned (response rate 42 per cent). The research established significant gaps in information about older carers, particularly older BME carers.

Gillies, B. (2000) 'Acting up: Role ambiguity and the legal recognition of carers', *Ageing and Society*, vol 20, pp 429-444.
This is a study of role ambiguity in carers of people with dementia. Ambiguity was seen to attach to: the needs of carers, their relationships with formal services, and their skills and experiences as carers. Twenty people with dementia were interviewed and their respective carers were then sampled opportunistically and interviewed (separately where possible). Coding was performed *post hoc* and based on grounded theory principles. Respondent-led thematic analysis was then performed on the interview findings. Role ambiguity is seen to permeate the relationship between formal and informal care.

Goss, S. and Miller, C. (1995) *From margin to mainstream*, York: Joseph Rowntree Foundation.
This article is probably the second most commonly applied typology of how to embrace and foster user and carer involvement. As the title suggests, carers should be in the mainstream rather the periphery of service planning and provision.

Halliday, B. and Dixon, P. (1996) 'Perceptions of care management within a Northern Ireland health and social services board', *Elders: The Journal of Care and Practice*, vol 5, no 3, pp 20-28.
This Northern Ireland study was based on face to-face interviews with service users (*n*=171) and carers (*n*=90) sampled randomly but with a selection review process that ensured that the carers of older people, disabled people and people with mental health problems were represented in the sample. All interviewees had experienced the care management process. Carers were generally satisfied with their care packages, with 74% stating that they had been consulted about them. This research is based on those known to the care boards of Northern Ireland and does not explore the extent and reasons for non-contact with health and social care bodies.

Hanson, E., Tetley, J. and Clarke, A. (1999) 'A multimedia intervention to support family caregivers', *Gerontologist*, vol 39, no 6, pp 736-741.
This technical report details a multimedia approach to enhancing family carers' support needs. The project – under the auspices of the European Union Action Programme – uses telematic applications and iterative work with carers to establish computer-based respite and long-term care choices. A range of research methods underpin the study, including an ethnographic decision-making scheme, user trials and focus group interviews. The programme of research has been peer-reviewed and is replicable in other country contexts. The user trials involved four professionals and four carers. However, it is unclear from the research findings what the quantifiable pay-offs will be for carers.

Harding, R. and Higginson, I. (2003) 'What is the best way to help caregivers in cancer and palliative care? A systematic literature review of interventions and their effectiveness', *Palliative Medicine*, vol 17, no 17, pp 63-74.
This clinical meta-study looked at the types of reported interventions in a systematically reviewed literature of supportive interventions for informal carers in home-based palliative care arrangements. The effectiveness of each intervention was appraised. Interventions from articles (*n*=22) were identified from Medline, CancerLit, PsycINFO and Cinahl databases. Studies of intervention efficacy ranged from randomised control trials through to group research. Current understanding adds to our grasp of the range of possible interventions to reduce morbidity in informal carers, but more needs to be done to understand the outcomes and efficacy of the impact of intervention on carers. Informal peer support was one cited benefit given by carers in the studies of rural caring, while the article notes that the provision of support may sometimes be a negative development if it is imposed crudely and does not take account of the current self-reliance and self-perception of carers.

Hardy, B., Young, R. and Wistow, G. (1999) 'Dimensions of choice in the assessment and care management process: The views of older people, carers and care managers', *Health and Social Care in the Community*, vol 7, no 6, pp 483-491.
Choice is at the heart of this study of four LA settings (one shire county and three metropolitan districts). It interviewed 28 older service users, 20 informal carers

and 22 care managers to establish the levels of choice being exercised and in which service areas. The LAs were purposively sampled as they formed part of a DH 'Mixed Economy of Care' research programme. A mixture of focus groups, user case file analysis and face-to-face interviews formed the research design. Overall carers felt that they were consulted rather than involved, and there was some carer uncertainty as to what they could reasonably expect in terms of involvement and amount of service.

Heenan, D. (2000) 'Informal care in farming families in Northern Ireland: Some considerations for social work', *British Journal of Social Work,* **vol 30, no 6, pp 855-866.**
This paper addresses carer issues and family care dynamics in rural Northern Ireland. The article, based on a literature review of informal care, forms the core of the research. It reveals the urban bias of much research to date and the need to account for rural carers as potential 'hidden' carers. Carer and user reciprocity was also a key feature of the research, which may challenge burden theories of caring.

Henderson, J. (2001) '"He's not my carer – he's my husband": Personal and policy constructions of care in mental health', *Journal of Social Work Practice,* **vol 15, no 2, pp 149-160.**
This largely conceptual study explored partners' constructions of care for carers and service users with a diagnosis of manic depression (bipolar disorder). Twenty-one people were interviewed using a semi-structured approach (carer *n*=11), and the interview findings were shared and confirmed by participants. Views on caring were compared and discourses analysed. Henderson counsels caution in assuming shared meanings about care and the need to question the theoretical premises of partnership working.

Henderson, J. and Forbat, L. (2002) 'Relationship-based social policy: Personal and policy constructions of "care"', *Critical Social Policy,* **vol 22, no 4, pp 665-683.**
This conceptual article critically explores the perceived absence of 'emotional labour' in the caring relationship and its absence from the national carers' strategy. Examples of the theoretical exploration can be found in the two studies carried out by the authors (one per author). The first explored the construction difficulties in the caring relationship of 12 carers (middle and working class, white British and Asian, heterosexual and homosexual relationships). The second study was of carers for people with a diagnosis of bipolar disorder. Again an ethnic and social class mix were evident in the participant profile. It is unclear in the latter study how the 21 people studied were divided into groups of carers and service users. Both studies used semi-structured interviews. By listening to partner constructions of caring, the emotional labour of caring becomes obvious – something the authors see as absent in the 1999 carers' strategy.

Hepworth, D. (2002) *Improving assessment and support for South Asian carers,* **York: Sir Halley Stewart Trust/Social Policy Research Unit, University of York.**
This study explored how CASI and CADI were tested with South Asian carers to appraise their cultural sensitivities and applicability of use with other South Asian carers. Carers were recruited using non-random method and through local carer

support centres. The tools were made available in Gujurati and Urdu. These tools had previously been applied with (mainly) white carers. Follow-up group meetings also added to the insights gained. Carers (*n*=26) found the tests applied well. A secondary aim of the research was to assist LAs in improving their assessment working with Asian carers.

Heron, C. (1998) *Working with carers*, London: Jessica Kingsley Publishing.
This conceptual and reflective book offers a comprehensive, if now slightly dated, appraisal of professional good practice when working with carers and draws on some brief but helpful empirical carer commentaries (of unclear origins and research methods). Notwithstanding the methodological limitations, this is a useful text exploring a range of practice standards and improvement tools for working in partnership with carers.

Jarvis, A. and McIntosh, G. (2004) 'The recognition and support of carers', *Professional Nurse*, vol 20, no 4, pp 24-26.
This evaluative study aimed to assess the impact of employing a CSDW. A pilot project involved the CSDW in raising GP awareness of carer needs to help identify 'hidden' carers and to enhance multiagency working to support carers. Carers' views were garnered (*n*=45, data collection method unstated) during the referral process and hidden carers were identified. Carers were clear about their need for more information, involvement and education, particularly as it relates to understanding mental health problems. Although hidden carers were a focus of this study, it is unclear how this fact specifically shaped the research findings.

Katbamna, S., Ahmad, W., Bhaktar, P., Barker, R. and Parker, G. (2004) 'Do they look after their own? Informal support in South Asian families', *Health and Social Care in the Community*, vol 12, no 5, pp 398-406.
This study confirmed earlier findings (SSI, Welsh Assembly) that debunked the notion that South Asians look after their own and therefore need little in the way of support. Both male and female carers (*n*=105) from Punjabi, Sikh, Gujarati, Hindu and Bangladeshi communities were asked about the extent of available community support. There was little, and the large close-knit communities assumed in much community care policy were also absent. Greater support and ethnic involvement in planning and responding to care needs is required.

Keeley, B. and Clarke, M. (2002) *Carers speak out*, London: PRT.
This research review of the efficacy of the carers' strategy was undertaken three years after it was introduced. It is a survey of 8,000 carers (with responses from 2,800 carers) in England, Wales and Scotland contacted through the Princess Royal Trust for Carers network. Postal survey questionnaires were complemented by a series of 12 national carer consultation meetings that attracted 1,000 carers (data collection method unstated). The latter provided the ideas, issues and concerns that formed the basis of a good practice guide to consultation with carers. The research also aimed to contact otherwise 'hidden' carers. While the exact method of achieving this was not spelt out, BME carers did represent 8% of survey respondents. Inconsistency of carer information and assessment are key messages of this study.

Kersten, P. (2001) 'Needs of carers of severely disabled people: Are they identified and adequately met?', *Health and Social Care in the Community*, **vol 5, no 4, pp 235-243.**

This study – a mixture of conceptual and empirical work – examined the views about carers' needs of 'severely' disabled service users, professionals and carers themselves. Using the Southampton Needs Assessment Questionnaire (SNAQ) to explore carer, user and professional perceptions of needs, 53 matched users, carers and professionals (mainly GPs) were identified and findings compared. Carers' health status was also measured using the SF 36 protocol. The research found that carers' needs were poorly recognised by service users and professionals alike. Short breaks proved to be the area in which carer perceptions of need far outstripped user and professional perceptions of the same need.

Last, A. (2003) 'User involvement: Pick and choose', *Health Service Journal*, **vol 113, no 5852, pp 28-29.**

This article details an initiative to involve carers in selection interviews for a lead officer post in learning disabilities. Both the local PCT and SSD, which had a history of carer involvement, would be jointly responsible for the appointment. Involvement in the selection of a key care manager would be a step further in the involvement process. Three user and three carer groups (*n*=6 in total) were contacted and asked to nominate a representative for the interview selection panel. Two users and four carers were eventually put forward for the panel. The involvement of users with learning difficulties and carers proved very useful, although the researchers noted the need for adequate lead time and training of panel members if involvement and fair recruitment are both to be achieved.

Lelliott, P., Beevor, A., Hogman, G., Hyslop, J., Lathlean, J. and Ward, M. (2003) 'Carers' and users' expectations of services – carer version (cues-c): A new instrument to support the assessment of carers of people with severe mental illness', *Journal of Mental Health*, **vol 12, no 2, pp 143-152.**

This technical psychiatric appraisal of a carer assessment tool aimed to ground a revised carer assessment tool in terms of what carers of people with 'severe' mental illness felt was important. The non-randomised test called C-CUES was piloted on 412 carers, and 75 of them provided structured feedback (of an unspecified nature) on the C-CUES assessment method. Retest reliability measures suggest that the tool is reliable and that, although largely for clinical use, it may have wider value in mental health settings where carer needs and risks are being appraised.

Lister, S., Mitchell, W., Sloper, W. and Roberts, K. (2003) 'Participation and partnerships in research: Listening to the ideas and experiences of a parent-carer', *International Journal of Social Research Methodology*, **vol 6, no 2, pp 159-165.**

This article appraises a carer's experiences of involvement in three research projects that largely revolved around family and carer needs for families with disabled or chronically sick children. Lister reflects both on his own and the wider research population's experiences of research and makes recommendations for carer and user-inclusive research in future studies. Lister *et al* point to the need for carer/user input on research location, continuity of setting, accessibility issues, finding a neutral setting for research, and guaranteeing research participants privacy. The overall observation that carer participants should be listened to was a key message of the study.

Lloyd, M. and Carson, A. (2005) 'Culture shift: Carer empowerment and cooperative inquiry', *Journal of Psychiatric and Mental Health Nursing*, **vol 12, no 2, pp 187-191.**

This action research study involved carers being enabled to develop an information pack for others based on their identified needs and narrative exchanges with clinical professionals. A cooperative inquiry approach (Heron and Reason, 2001) was adopted as the basis of the research partnership. Initial use of a questionnaire formulated by carer support workers was found to be inadequate in focus and inappropriate in the use of complex language (with only a 5% response rate). In Phase 1 of the study, meetings were held with carers (*n*=3, no carer numbers specified) to explore issues of greatest importance. These became the basis of the revised research (Phase 2). A follow-up meeting was held (Phase 3) to validate findings, and Phase 4 involved a joint report with carers on outcomes, as well as the development of an information pack. The pack was designed to steer carers through available resources and agency support. It is unclear how power sharing translated into an iterative action research process.

McGarry, J. and Arthur, A. (2001) 'Informal caring in late life: A qualitative study of the experiences of older carers', *Journal of Advanced Nursing*, **vol 33, no 2, pp 182-189.**

Older carers (>75) were interviewed to explore their experiences of providing spousal and sibling care. Fourteen interviews (13 spousal carers and one sibling carer) took place, based on opportunist sampling taking GP health check patients as the basis of the research population. Systematic qualitative data analysis was employed using co-researcher verification. The continued preference of informal over formal support, uncertainty over service availability and constraints on visiting GPs (the screening tool for this review) were all factors militating against greater carer support.

Macgregor, M. and Hill, M. (2003) *Missed opportunities: The impact of new rights for carers*, **London: Carers UK.**

This study evaluated the views of carers on their experiences of care support services in the light of the Carers Act 1995, the 1999 carers' strategy and the Carers and Disabled Children Act 2000. A specific focus of the research was that of carer assessment. In all, 1,695 carers in England responded to a postal survey. A separate but complementary survey of 10 English LAs' responses to policy changes was also despatched. Only 32% of carers surveyed had received an assessment, a small rise on similar research conducted in 1997, when it was 21%.

McKeown, L., Porter-Armstrong, A. and Baxter, G. (2003) 'The needs and experiences of caregivers of individuals with multiple sclerosis: A systemic review', *Clinical Rehabilitation*, **vol 17, no 3, pp 234-248.**

This article relates a systematic review of the needs and experiences of caregivers of people with MS. The following computerised databases were searched between 1990 and 2002: Cinahl, BIDS, IBSS, ASSIA, Medline, PsycINFO, British Nursing Index, ISI Web of Knowledge, Zetoc and AMED. Twenty-four studies met the inclusion criteria. Findings suggest the need for enhanced professional work with carers, including the need to monitor and encourage community supports and to review the needs of carers of people with MS regularly.

Manthorpe, J. (2000) 'Developing carers' contributions to social work training', *Social Work Education*, vol 19, no 1, pp 19-27.
This article took the form of a conceptual exploration of models of carer involvment in social work training. Manthorpe identifies three models of carer involvement: personal testimony, carer as co-trainer, and use of social work students and sessional staff's own perceptions of caring. The risks and benefits of each model are examined. Manthorpe, although inconclusive as to the best model to embrace, acknowledges the complexity of carer issues and the importance of carer and user involvement.

Manthorpe, J. (2003) 'Nearest and dearest? The neglect of lesbians in caring relationships', *British Journal of Social Work*, vol 33, no 6, pp 753-768.
This theoretical and conceptual article explores the neglect of lesbian carers and providing service equity that takes their needs into account. It argues that a heterosexual construction of caring is assumed even in partner research and policy on carers. The article raises points of central importance to inclusive participatory working with lesbian (and gay) carers' needs.

Manthorpe, J. and Twigg, J. (1995) 'Carers and care management', *Baseline*, vol 59, pp 4-8.
This study of two LAs (one urban, the other a mix of urban and rural populations) aimed to draw out developments in carer participation – in particular, current articulations of 'needs' and 'rights' in the context of carer policy. This is effectively a case study approach that looks at two contrasting authorities at different stages of implementing carer participation policy at a local level. However, neither had very clear ideas about just what needs and rights substantively meant, for example, in terms of assessment of carers.

Manthorpe, J., Alaszewski, A., Gates, B., Ayer, S. and Motherby, A. (2003) 'Learning disability nursing: User and carer perceptions', *Journal of Learning Disabilities*, vol 7, no 2, pp 119-135.
This study focused on carer and user perceptions of learning disability nursing and was oriented to enhancing nurse education to respond more fully to user and carer needs. Eight focus groups were held, which encapsulated the views of carers, people with learning difficulties and their wider families. Issues about learning difficulty nursing included awareness of nursing staff and their role, and involvement-related issues such as 'Have you been involved in nurse education?' (based on Arnstein's ladder of participation). The focus groups were based on established community and voluntary groups. Verbatim transcriptions were made of the focus group discussions. Carers and users felt learning difficulty nurses could do more to raise their profile by, for example, joining local voluntary groups. There was only one instance of consultation noted in the research. Closer professional and user/carer working in education and training was a key finding.

Middleton, T. (2001) 'Mental health services for older people: Towards an integrated approach', *Mental Health Review*, vol 6, no 2, pp 22-24.
This article relates the development of an integrated mental health strategy in South East England. This drew on the experiences of one carer from a local Alzheimer's group, whose experiences and insights were fed into the development of the strategy. The wider Alzheimer's group membership of carers and service users were to be consulted at a later date. Carer involvement was seen to add validity to the strategy.

Milne, A. (2004) 'Culture and care in dementia', *Updates: Research and policy briefings from the Mental Health Foundation,* **vol 5, no 5.**
This action research study, part of the 'Culture and Care Dementia' project, set out to examine the service-related needs and deficits of Asian people and their carers (*n*=unstated) in North West Kent. Cultural barriers included assumptions that dementia was a natural part of ageing, and service barriers limited access to culturally sensitive services.

Mitchell, F. (1996) 'Carer support groups', *Practice,* **vol 8, no 4, pp 53-59.**
This was a study of carer support interventions by professionals working in six carer support groups. Mitchell tested previous research that had found little impact of professional or peer-led support (Toseland, Rossiter and Labreque, 1989). The groups were categorised as: day centres for disabled people, free-standing generic groups open to carers of all client groups, free-standing specific groups (stroke support and BME group). The multistage study involved (non-participant? not specified) observations at the six day centres and follow-up interviews with 18 carers (three from each centre) and six professionals. Follow-up observations were completed to measure the professional impact effect. The study concludes that professional involvement can make a 'significant and distinctive contribution' (measurement not specified) – for example, in making carers aware of their rights and, for some, in reflecting on the fact that they are carers.

Molyneux, J. and Irvine, J. (2004) 'Service user and carer involvement in social work training: A long and winding road?', *Social Work Education,* **vol 23, no 4, pp 293-308.**
This study appraised the current and potential future involvement of users and carers in social work education and training. Using a convenient or opportunist sampling method, 17 individuals and groups were studied, although the exact breakdown of these participants is unclear. Face-to-face research evinced views of how carers and users can be more involved in social work training and education. Carer and user diversity was noted – in particular, BME carers – but it is unclear how this impacted on the research design.

Newbronner, E. and Hare, P. (2002) *Services to support carers of people with mental health problems: Consultation report for the National Coordinating Centre for NHS Service Delivery and Organisation RandD (NCCSDO),* **York: University of York.**
This NHS (NCCSDO) study researched the support services available for carers of people with mental health problems. Key stakeholder consultations (method unstated) with national and local statutory and voluntary-sector organisations was complemented with key informant carer consultations (discussion groups or telephone interviews: *n*=unstated). The carer comments were used to check the appropriateness of earlier professional commentary – for example, good practice examples, notions of service effectiveness. A framework technique (Ritchie and Spencer, 1994) was used to analyse the data collected. Insufficient time and money disallowed the inputting of supplementary data from 84 service organisations' best practice.

Nichol, M., Ashworth, M., McNally, L. and Newman, S. (2002) 'Satisfaction with respite care: A pilot study', *Health and Social Care in the Community*, vol 10, no 6, pp 479-484.
This is a pilot study of carers who are looking after dependants with dementia. It aimed to explore whether wider social supports enhanced positive experiences of respite care. Twenty-six carers (from 140 contacted) completed questionnaires. Satisfaction measures were based on 'previously validated scales', and the study suggested that the presence of a wider social network was significant in enhancing satisfaction with respite care (correlation coefficient).

Nicholas, E. (2003) 'An outcome focus in carer assessment and review: Value and challenge', *British Journal of Social Work*, vol 33, no 1, pp 31-48.
This project-based study tested practice-based tools to enhance and promote carer-centred practice. The project, which focused on the process and outcomes of carer involvement, had two phases. Phase 1 involved the use of interviews and focus groups to explore what older people, younger disabled people, carers and practitioners/managers felt about outcomes. Views on preferred outcomes formed the basis of Phase 2, which saw the roll-out of outcomes measures in one LA (no control group or comparator methodology). The outcomes approach focused on the experiences of carers of older people. Trial implementation involved 14 practitioners working with older people's assessments (n=37). Fifteen assessment follow-ups were completed. Significant gains and challenges were attached to the use of outcome tools.

Noble, D. and Bateman, N. (1995) *Respite – The way forward in Kent*, Canterbury: Kent Action for Respite Choice/Kent Social Services/East Kent Health Authority.
This six-part 1993 national study of respite care provision and shortfall was undertaken by Kent Social Services, East Kent Health Authority and West Kent Health Authority. It aimed to arrive at an understanding of respite, particularly as it impacts carers of disabled people. It included a literature review, a national survey of respite providers and a number of surveys centred on Kent: respite providers, leisure providers, 'innovative agencies' (defined as disability-led), and disabled people and carers. No respondent numbers are specified for any of the above, nor are data triangulation methods discussed. Inadequate respite care, poor awareness of respite options and the need for greater multiagency working and carer involvement were noted.

Nolan, M. (2001) 'Working with family carers: Towards a partnership approach', *Reviews in Clinical Gerontology*, vol 11, pp 91-97.
This article is a conceptual reflection on the implications of implementing a partnership approach to caring in a rehabilitation context. Following Twigg and Atkin (*Carers perceived: Policy and practice in informal care*, 1994 – see below), Nolan explores different models or professional perceptions of carers and the implications of these constructions for carer support. Nolan advocates a wholesale embracing of 'carers as experts' if professionals are to support carers in making informed choices.

Nolan, M., Grant, G. and Keady, J. (1996) *Understanding family care: A multidisciplinary model of caring and coping*, Buckingham: Open University Press.
This book explores conceptually the changing meaning and experience of caring. The research on which it is based examines the complex relationships between carers and

those cared for and their needs. It is an amalgam of data sources and pre-existing studies by the authors – including several hundred structured interviews, three large-scale postal surveys, participant and non-participant observation – and would repay a complete reading. The book itself looks in detail at studies of carer satisfaction, and carers' coping strategies. (The fieldwork for the study of carer satisfaction and reciprocity predates this review but is available: Grant, G. and Nolan, M. [1993] 'Informal carers: Sources and concomitants of satisfaction', *Health and Social Care in the Community*, vol 1, no 3.)

Nolan, M., Grant, G. and Keady, J. (1998) *Assessing the needs of family carers: A guide for practitioners*, Brighton: Pavilion.
This guide for practitioners includes an exploration of the value and operationalisation of an outcomes framework – 'carers indices' – to aid in more successfully identifying positive carer outcomes. The indices are based on carer-friendly formulations using a series of (*n*=3) questionnaires containing 36 rating statements to evince the challenges and satisfactions of caring and the best way for care management to respond to these insights.

Nolan, M., Ingram, P. and Watson, R. (2002) 'Working with family carers of people with dementia: "Negotiated" coping as an essential outcome', *Dementia: The Journal of Social Research and Practice*, vol 1, no 1, pp 75-93.
Although an Australian dataset is used, the direct application and comparison with carers' experiences in the UK makes this research worthy of inclusion. Completed questionnaires on carers coping while caring for someone with dementia were received from 156 family carers using non-random self-selecting sampling methods. The findings then are illustrative and not generalisable. The research makes the often-cited point that, while a repertoire of coping strategies is in use, an ongoing issue is the need to adopt an emancipatory approach to acknowledging the expertise of carers as a basis for greater partnerships.

Olsen, R., Parker, G. and Drewett, A. (1997) 'Carers and the missing link: Changing professional attitudes', *Health and Social Care in the Community*, vol 5, no 2, pp 116-123.
This paper is based on a literature mapping project of then current service development for carers. The involvement and consultation with carers in this development is appraised. National and local carer projects that had been evaluated were gathered together to provide a full, if not systematic, review of carer involvement activity. Published work was collated to provide a picture of carers' involvement. While involvement is increasing, key challenges remain: (a) reaching 'hidden' carers (and getting carers to identify themselves as such); (b) distinguishing, in academic or service reviews of involvement, between the quantity and quality of involvement; (c) giving more attention to the outcomes of involvement; (d) overcoming the difficulties of collectively representing carers; and (e) ensuring that strategic policies filter down to street level.

Pickard, L. (2001) 'Carer break or carer-blind? Policies for informal carers in the UK', *Social Policy and Administration*, vol 35, no 4, pp 441-458.
This article is a policy evaluation of three policy documents that have had a major impact on carer policy and practice developments: the national strategy for carers

document, the report of the Royal Commission on Long-term Care, and the note of dissent to the majority of the commission's findings. The implications of the different premises of the documents for carer empowerment are made clear.

Pickard, S., Jacobs, S. and Kirk, S. (2003) 'Challenging professional roles: Lay carer's involvement in health care in the community', *Social Policy and Administration,* **vol 37, no 1, pp 82-96.**
This research evaluated and compared three carer projects: one involving older carers of older people (*n*=24), another with parent carers of 'technology-dependent' children (38), and a third involving home care (paid) workers (15). Semi-structured interviews and focus group methods were used with carers and professionals to aid understanding of the different perspectives on the professional role in supporting carers. Cross-group comparisons were made between unpaid and paid carers.

Powell, E. (2002) *We care too: A good practice guide for people working with black carers,* **London: Afiya Trust/National Black Carers Workers Network.**
This good practice guide is based on the brief comments of BME carers and care workers on their perceptions of service provision for carers and the best forms of responses to any deficits. Although these comments are not gleaned using formal academic conventions, this report has been included because BME care voices are significantly under-represented in the literature, and while 'official voices' fail to capture BME narratives, this seems acceptable in formulating a service and policy response. The main conclusion is that the power imbalance in 'black and white citizenry' needs to be addressed if power sharing can happen substantively in care services.

Preston-Shoot, M. (2003) 'Only connect: Client, carer and professional perspectives on community care assessment processes', *Research, Policy and Planning,* **vol 21, no 3, pp 23-35.**
This article draws on findings from a perception audit of two research projects that focuses on the perspectives of users, carers and professionals on service needs and the extent to which these needs were met. Clients and carers were also asked about their level of satisfaction with services. Formative focus groups and interviews were the research methods adopted in both projects, and the views of carers, clients and professionals were compared and triangulated. Research populations varied slightly between projects, and the sample sizes were 76 (Buckley, Preston-Shoot and Smith, 1995) and 46 (Preston-Shoot and Wigley, 1999). According to this article by Preston-Shoot, key differences in professional, client and carer perception are likely to make partnership working a real challenge in the future.

Princess Royal Trust (2003) *Focus on carers and the NHS: Identifying and supporting hidden carers – Good practice guide,* **London: PRT.**
This article details an initiative conducted in Scotland, but as it deals with the issue of 'hidden' carers, it was seen as having a wider value and replicability in the UK more generally. A 'carers and NHS good practice guide' was the main aim of the initiative. Partnership is the key focus of this work, which contains good practice examples of where carer and health services are working well in partnership. Alongside the development of the guide, the trust worked in primary care settings to identify carers by means of a brief questionnaire survey (sampling unstated). A range of methods

were used to encourage carers to come forward. As the report of the initiative states: 'This working partnership has helped to highlight and validate the carer's role'.

Qureshi, H., Bamford, C., Nicholas, E., Patmore, C. and Harris, J. (2000) *Implementing an outcomes approach to carer assessment and review: Social Policy Research Unit report for the Department of Health*, **York: Social Policy Research Unit.**

This study was focused on carers of older people and the development of an outcomes framework and tools for carer assessment and review. The tools and framework were shaped by carers, front-line staff and managers in one English SSD. The tools were tested on volunteers (*n*=14) and social care workers (*n*=9 social workers, 5 home care coordinators) in both community and hospital contexts. First, carers (*n*=37) were given an assessment, and Stage 2 saw them (*n*=15) being reviewed to provide outcomes evidence. BME carers were included (*n*=6) in the carer assessment sample. A carers reference group and in-depth interviews with all staff and with a sample of the carers' (*n*=unstated) were also features of the evaluation. Both professionals and carers felt that their understanding of care needs had increased, and the professionals' views suggested that they had got a clearer sense of what carers need through outcomes tools. However, gaining carers' views was more time-consuming than had been anticipated.

Rethink (2003) *Who cares? The experiences of mental health carers accessing services and information*, **London: Rethink.**

This study explored the experiences of mental health carers seeking support and information. Both service users and carers were surveyed using an indirect mailing method, and 1,451 postal questionnaires, which asked both closed and open-ended questions, were returned by carer. The carers contacted were known to Rethink and their partner organisations so the responses may be under-representative of 'hidden' or disaffected carers. Although overall perceptions were that services for people with mental health problems were improving in 2003, the levels of involvement of carers was viewed as limited and fell short of what many carers viewed as partnerships with professionals. Patient confidentiality was a specific factor that limited this.

Rhodes, P. and Shaw, S. (1999) 'Informal care and terminal illness', *Health and Social Care in the Community*, **vol 7, no 1, pp 39-50.**

A study in one Yorkshire health authority of 33 largely family carers who had been bereaved (in previous 18 months), this research looked at the role and function of support to both the dying person and the carer. In-depth interviews were held with bereaved carers, who were selected by sex and geographical spread from one year's death certificates to reflect wider population profiles. Palliative care and wider support provision was patchy and the changing nature of formerly industrial and settled communities raised issues for future patterns of informal caring where inevitable family mobility may reduce the informal networks on which palliative support is based.

Robinson, C. and Williams, V. (2002) 'Carers of people with learning disabilities, and their experience of the 1995 Carers Act', *British Journal of Social Work*, **vol 32, no 2, pp 169-183.**

In Phase 1 of this three-phase study of carers of people with learning difficulties, researchers interviewed senior managers in 15 LA/SSDs and associated health trusts to establish which carer policies were in place. Phase 2 involved a records search of carer assessments in five LAs to discover the number undertaken in the year leading up to the study. This led to 20 interviews with carers who had been assessed in that year. Phase 3 saw follow-up interviews with 18 carers and (matched) service users with learning disabilities who had experienced 'significant change' during the lifetime of the research. It was found that the Carers Act 1995 had made little impact on the number of assessments in the locality.

Rogers, H. (1996) 'Breaking the ice: Developing strategies for collaborative working with carers of older people with mental health problems', in H. Kemshall and R. Littlewood (eds) (2000) *User involvement and participation in social care*, London: Jessica Kingsley Publishing.
This two-stage community-based action research study of carers of older people with mental health problems was situated in the older people's directorate of a Midlands mental health NHS trust. In Stage 1, a questionnaire using open and closed questions was despatched to carers, followed by a series of focus groups. In all, 66 carers responded to the questionnaire and 42 agreed to take part in the groups. The questionnaire and the focus group invitation were part of an information pack that aimed both to secure research involvement and to let carers know why the older people's directorate wanted to work more closely with carers. Stages 2 and 3, based on the findings of the survey and the focus groups, took the form of service responses to concerns raised, including psycho-educational sessions on dementia and attempts to reduce GP–consultant referral delays.

Royal College of Nursing/Unison (2004) *Not 'just' a friend: Best practice on health care guidance for lesbian, gay and bisexual service users and their families*, London: Royal Colllege of Nursing.
This is a best practice guide for health service workers working with LGB patients, their families and carers. Best practice examples have been gleaned opportunistically to provide illustrations of best practice with LGB people, their partners and families. The guide is focused largely on user needs, but has clear implications for involving carers in care settings.

Rummery, K., Ellis, K. and Davis, A. (1999) 'Negotiating access to community care assessments: Perspectives of front-line workers, people with disability and carers', *Health and Social Care in the Community*, vol 7, no 4, pp 296-300.
This multimethod study involved observations of carer assessment practice in two LA/SSDs (six teams). In-depth interviews were also undertaken with 50 disabled service users and 23 carers. The two social work settings were selected for their population diversity: one had an urban population with a 9.7% BME population profile; the other was a mixed urban/rural area with a 3.4% BME profile. Sample weighting for age, disability and ethnicity was completed. Some five years after the Carers Act 1995, there were still problems for carers getting assessments.

Ryan, T. and Bamber, C. (2002) 'A survey of policy and practice on expenses and other payments to mental health service users and carers participating in service delivery', *Journal of Mental Health*, vol 11, no 6, pp 635-644.
Ryan and Bamber undertook a study of 41 organisations using a questionnaire survey, in which they explored the use and perception of expenses payments. Organisations surveyed included NHS trusts and health authorities, SSDs and 'other' organisations.

Carer participation was central to this study, and key ways in which organisations support carer involvement were delineated. Most respondent organisations had payment protocols in place and were paying carer expenses, but there was a system to these payments was generally lacking and there was little involvement of carers in formulating payment schemes.

Scott, G., Whyler, N. and Grant, G. (2001) 'A study of family carers of people with a life-threatening illness 1: The carers' needs analysis', *International Journal of Palliative Nursing*, **vol 7, no 6, pp 290-291.**
This nursing study aimed to examine the support needs of carers of people with life-threatening illnesses. A total of 24 carers from a Macmillan nursing team database were asked to take part in a qualitative study. Following interviews with them, a simple content analysis was undertaken to establish the patterns of responses. The stress experienced by carers and the need for intensive professional support were identified as key issues in the research, and the carer's age, gender and length of time as a carer were all seen as important factors when planning support.

Seddon, D. (1999) 'Negotiating caregiving and employment', in S. Cox and J. Keady (eds) *Younger people with dementia: Planning, practice and development*, **London: Jessica Kingsley Publishing.**
This article looks at the increasingly important area of worker carers having to juggle both paid employment and informal caring. The psychological and physical health of carers and their moving between work and being on benefits were all seen as challenges. The need for greater involvement in service planning and delivery is significant here but, in the short term, presents a dilemma for a group of carers who may, in addition to their paid work, have wider family responsibilities beyond caring and little time for airing their concerns in a partnership context.

Seddon, D. and Robinson, C. (2001) 'Carers of older people with dementia: Assessment and the Carers Act', *Health and Social Care in the Community*, **vol 9, no 3, pp 151-158.**
This three-phase study evaluated the process and outcomes of carer assessments. Phase 1 involved 23 strategic semi-structured telephone interviews with senior social services staff; Phase 2 entailed 32 semi-structured interviews with care managers; and Phase 3 comprised 64 in-depth semi-structured carer interviews of carers of older people with dementia. All selected carers had been assessed in the previous six months. Some six years after the accession of the Carers Act 1995, staff and carers remained unclear about the framework and basis on which carer assessment was being made.

Seddon, D. and Robinson, C. (2004) 'Supporting carers in paid work', *Working with Older People*, **vol 8, no 2, pp 13-18.**
This action-oriented study aimed to raise awareness of working carers' needs. Some 200 employers were surveyed via postal questionnaires, 40 LA employees were interviewed by telephone and 46 carers were interviewed face to face. Working carers' needs were not fully recognised by employers or statutory agencies. Carer assessments rarely took paid employment responsibilities into account. There was little evidence of multi agency working. The report aimed to stimulate interest in multi-agency work to support working carers.

Simon, C., Kumar, S. and Kendrick, T. (2002) 'Who cares for the carers? The district nurse perspective', *Family Practice*, **vol 19, no 1, pp 29-35.**
Following a postal survey (respondent numbers not stated) of district nurses' views of their role in supporting informal carers to access respite care, Simon, Kumar and Kendrick undertook a qualitative analyses of the 'open-ended' responses to establish the key messages of the study. District nurses were aware of the need to support carers in respite care – for example, by providing information and/or improved respite care. However, they saw GPs as better placed to offer primary support and signposting to better respite services.

Simon, C., Little, P., Birtwistle, J. and Kendrick, T. (2003) 'A questionnaire to measure satisfaction with community services for informal carers of stroke patients: Construction and initial piloting', *Health and Social Care in the Community*, **vol 11, no 2, pp 129-137.**
This clinical study relates how the researchers developed and piloted satisfaction measures for carers of stroke patients, using convenience sampling. The study was in two parts: first, the generation of satisfaction-scoping measures (numbers were unstated; each interview lasted 40 minutes); second, the development of Likert scale-based questions of satisfaction (based on the themes identified in part one) and the testing of the measure by 44 carers. Fixed-choice questionnaires were administered face-to-face by the research team (10 minutes per carer). The research authors felt the tests were valid and reliable, but needed testing on a larger research cohort before active use.

Simpson, A. (1999) 'Creating alliances: The views of users and carers on the education and training needs of community mental health nurses', *Journal of Psychiatric and Mental Health Nursing*, **vol 6, no 5, pp 347-356.**
This research was based on a development project using users' and carers' views that aims to identify and enhance the education and training needs of CMHN. A total of 52 service users and their representatives and 24 carers and other support workers were interviewed using semi-structured protocols. Additionally, focused discussion groups were used to draw out these ideas. The findings point to the need for CMHNs to involve carers and users as fully as possible in care planning. Carers want more information and 'more explicit' (transparent?) communication between mental health professionals and carers.

Simpson, E. and House, A. (2003) 'User and carer involvement in mental health services: From rhetoric to science', *British Journal of Psychiatry*, **vol 183, pp 89-91.**
This conceptual article systematically explored the principles of user and carer involvement. The article makes clear the risks of failing to reflect on these if professionals are to build structures based on them. Stages of involvement include: deciding on main involvement goal, choosing mechanism(s) of involvement, identifying possible barriers and solutions, evaluating the outcomes of the project and the use of data to inform future practice.

Simpson, R. (1997) 'Carers as equal partners in care planning', *Journal of Psychiatric Mental Health Nursing*, **vol 4, no 5, pp 345-354.**
This pilot study appraised the possible value of joint care planning by professionals and carers and of keeping care planning documents in the carers' (and users'?) home. The enhanced potential for the carer role and the inclusion value of home-located

documents were both studied. Alongside professional notes, carers could enter diary notes for significant events. A total of 15 families took part in the study. Carer interviews were held before and after the care documentation was transferred. The data findings were analysed both quantitatively (average score rating schedules) and qualitatively (unspecified technique described as 'structured framework analysis'). Despite some early ethical concerns about confidentiality, the project proved beneficial to professionals and carers, although some improvements to the documents were felt to be needed.

Smith, F., Francis, S.-A., Gray, N., Denham, M. and Graffy, J. (2003) 'A multi-centre survey among informal carers who manage medication for older care recipients: Problems experienced and development of services', *Health and Social Care in the Community,* **vol 11, no 2, pp 138-145.**
This multicentre survey of informal carers who manage medication for older people involved four randomly (stratified) sampled health authorities in one region. Stratification aimed to mirror wider age demography. A key inclusion criterion was the administration of medicines to older people being cared for. Researchers ($n=25$) were selected to match carers and care recipients by ethnicity and first language preference. A total of 287 carers and service users were interviewed ($n=184$ carers). Concerns were raised about carers having to make clinical decisions and knowing little about identifying unwarranted side-effects.

Social Services Inspectorate (1998) *A matter of chance for carers? Inspection of local authority support for carers,* **London: DH.**
This study was integrally linked to the SSI's inspection of English LA responses to the *Modernisation agenda in social care.* This suite of research activity included care managers, service providers and service users and carers. Postal questionnaire responses were received from 110 service users and carers (matched?) who were involved in service planning across England. Additionally, interviews (face-to-face and telephone) were held with key LA stakeholders. Carer and service user involvement was seen to have improved, while partnership working with cognate agencies had also developed. However, the systematic involvement of users and carers was nowhere in evidence, and there was still a road to travel in embedding these views into a wider LA context.

Social Services Inspectorate (1999) *They look after their own, don't they? Inspection of community care services for black and ethnic minority older people,* **London: DH/SSI.**
The SSI inspection report is a major study of ethnicity and community care. It looked at eight LAs – two London boroughs, one shire county and five urban centres in the English North and Midlands – with significant BME concentrations, particularly black populations. The study identified and evaluated the measures that LAs had taken in responding to the care needs of people and BME, both users and carers. Although much work is beginning to be rolled out in response to their needs, the confidence of care/support providers and BME users and carers has to be addressed more substantially. Cultural assumptions about BME carer networks also need to be addressed if equity in social care and support are to be established.

Took, M. (1999) 'Involving service users and carers', *Journal of Psychiatric and Mental Health Nursing,* **vol 6, no 6, pp 485-487.**

This article reflects, at a conceptual level, on the benefits to be gleaned from carer (and user) involvement. Writing for a psychiatry and mental health nursing audience, Took presents a number of key conceptual gains of partnership nursing with carers and users, including valuing their expertise and partnership in supporting and ensuring therapeutic compliance. The article offers concrete examples of how carers and users can be more fully involved – for example, the payment of expenses and ensuring a depth of involvement in service planning and avoiding tokenism.

Turner, S. and Street, H. (1999) 'Assessing carers' training needs: A pilot enquiry', *Aging and Mental Health,* **vol 3, no 2, pp 173-178.**

This pilot study of carers' training needs used formative focus groups of carers (two groups) and social work and community psychiatric nurses (CPN) professionals (two groups). The ideas around training needs were then formulated into a semi-structured interview. A total of 30 carers were interviewed. Information needs and condition management for carers of people with dementia were key issues to come out of the research, which need to be built into future carer training.

Turner, P., Sheldon, F., Coles, C., Mountford, B., Hillier, R., Radawy, P. and Wee, B. (2000) 'Listening to and learning from the family carer's story: An innovative approach in interprofessional education', *Journal of Interprofessional Care,* **vol 14, no 4, pp 387-395.**

Turner *et al* have produced an action research study of carer involvement in palliative care workshops, designed to give a range of health and social care professionals insights into the carer experience. A specialist evaluator was employed as a non-participant observer to evaluate three workshops where carers were interviewed on their caring insights. Twenty-eight carers had taken part in the workshops, and of these, 12 attended a follow-up feedback session. Alongside this group feedback, professionals were asked to evaluate their experiences of the carer-involved workshops. Overall carer involvement was validating for carers and enhanced inter-professional insights. The study authors acknowledge that the fall off in carer involvement from 28 to 12 may suggest that their findings are more positive than a full cohort analysis might have been.

Twigg, J. and Atkin, K. (1994) *Carers perceived: Policy and practice in informal care,* **Buckingham: Open University Press.**

This book is based on a wide-ranging study of how carers and the 'service system' interact, how resources are allocated and what criteria are used to allocate them. The study also looked at the models that professionals used in understanding carers and how to work with them. The book makes a seminal point that the way carers are perceived impacts profoundly on how services are constructed. The study itself involved interviews (n=90) with carers who share a household with those they are caring for, in two areas of North East England, to ensure a range of corresponding types of service user. Semi-structured interviews with service users and managers (n=125) were undertaken in 46 health authority and 48 LA contexts.

Walker, E. and Dewar, B. (2001) 'How do we facilitate carers' involvement in decision-making?', *Journal of Advanced Nursing*, vol 34, no 3, pp 329-337.
This study of family carer involvement in a respite and assessment hospital setting aims to explore the extent and nature of this involvement. Key characteristics of involvement were also explored, which help take forward debates about the value of involvement in healthcare settings. Informal carers (*n*=20) and multidisciplinary clinical staff (*n*=29) were interviewed face to face about their experiences and views of partnership working with carers. Non-participant observations of team meetings and ward routine augmented interview findings. Markers of involvement were: shared information, inclusion in decision making and ready personal points of contact for carers. Levels of involvement varied significantly and could have been more systematically embedded in professional practice.

Ward, C. (2001) *Family matters: Counting families in*, London: DH.
This report highlights the perspectives of family carers of people with learning difficulties, in an attempt – as the subtitle suggests – to 'count families in'. The findings are based on a review of projects to support family carers of people with learning difficulties and a supporting literature review of policy, practice and the experiences of family carers and those they care for. A family carers subgroup was established to inform the review. The report lays out what needs to be be done to bridge carer expectations and current care realities.

Warner, L. and Wexler, S. (1998) *Eight hours a day and taken for granted: You just get on with it, don't you?*, London: Princess Royal Trust for Carers.
This quantitative postal survey study of carers (*n*=1,346) was completed three years after the passing to the Carers Act 1995, but before the *Caring for carers* strategy. The unmet needs of carers were significant. Carer contributions often went unrecognised, and, according to carers, most professionals were unaware of their needs. The report helped establish the need for a greater (and embedded) carer voice in service provision.

Welsh Assembly Government (2002) *Challenging the myth 'They look after their own': Black and minority ethnic (BME) carers*, Cardiff: WNA.
This research, prompted by the *'Caring about Carers' strategy – A carers' strategy for Wales*, examined whether services were accessible for Welsh carers. Three Welsh localities were identified for the study, and a range of research methods were used including a literature review (published and grey) and direct discussions with BME carers (*n*=43) from a range of carer types, including partner/spousal, adult carers and young carers. Additionally two focus groups were held for BME carers (*n*=13) in separate locations. The report highlighted a number of barriers to South Asian carers' recognition and support, including the need for culturally sensitive professionals and the end to assumptions that they 'care for their own'.

Wenger, G., Scott, A. and Seddon, D. (2002) 'The experience of caring for older people with dementia in a rural area: Using services', *Ageing and Mental Health*, vol 6, no 1, pp 30-38.
This study is part of a suite of research under the auspices of the Medical Research Centre (MRC) Multi-Centre Study of Cognitive Function and Ageing (CFAS). This research, informally known as the Gwynedd Study, involved an exploration of how

those caring for people with dementia have experienced carer support services. In Tranche 1, 28 carers were interviewed, with follow-up interviews with 18 of them in Tranche 2; a further 12 carers were added to the sample. The interviews were semi-structured and open-ended. Although receiving low levels of service, most carers were highly satisfied with what they did get. Yet carer assessments did not trigger automatically when dementia was recognised, while the stress of a carer was not embraced and responded to by much professional activity.

Woods, R., Wills, W., Higginson, I., Hobbins, J. and Whitby, M. (2003) 'Support in the community for people with dementia and their carers: A comparative outcome study of specialist mental health service interventions', *International Journal of Geriatric Psychiatry,* **vol 18, no 4, pp 298-307.**
Comparative research on carers of people with dementia, these carers being in receipt of Admiral Nursing Service (ANS) specialist support. A total of 128 carers were recruited to the study (55 in the ANS group, 73 in a comparator group). The ANS group was interviewed shortly after getting ANS support and then eight months later (n=104, attrition rate of 18.8%). There were no significant differences in stress levels across the two intervention approaches.

Yeandle, S., Crompton, R., Wigfield, A. and Dennet, J. (2002) *Employed carers and family-friendly policies,* **Joseph Rowntree Foundation, Bristol/York: The Policy Press/Joseph Rowntree Foundation.**
This study of working carers aimed to measure the burden of unpaid care done by working carers. The research involved a survey of 945 employers, case studies of 'family-friendly' employment policies, and interviews and focus groups with carers, service providers and employers in three sectors – retail banking, supermarkets, local government – in two geographical settings: Sheffield and Kent. Locality was seen as significant, particularly as regards the availability of support in caring, and there was an obvious gap between employer and carer awareness of family-friendly policies. Carer involvement in enhancing employers' awareness of their needs is a key finding of the study.

Appendix C: Databases searched

PubMed

#1 Carer particip*
#2 Carer AND particip*
#3 Carers AND particip*
#4 Caring AND particip*
#5 Caregiver AND particip*
#6 Carer AND assess*
#7 Carers AND assess*
#8 Caring AND assess*
#9 Caregiver AND assess*
#10 Carer AND plann*
#11 Carers AND plann*
#12 Caring AND plann*
#13 Caregiver AND plann*
#14 Carers WITH particip*
#15 Carers WITH particip*
#16 Caring WITH particip*
#17 Caregiver WITH particip*
#18 Carer WITH involve*
#19 Carers WITH involve*
#20 Caring WITH involve*
#21 Caregiver WITH involve*
#22 Carer WITH inclus*
#23 Carers WITH inclus*
#24 Caring WITH inclus*
#25 Caregiver WITH inclus*
#26 Carer AND plann*
#27 Carers AND Plann*
#28 Caring AND Plann*
#29 Caregiver AND Plann*
#30 Carer AND Review
#31 Carers AND Review
#32 Caring AND Review
#33 Caregiver AND Review
#34 Carer AND Partner*
#35 Carers AND Partner*
#36 Caring AND Partner*
#37 Caregiver AND Partner*
#38 Carer AND Agreem*
#39 Carers AND Agreem*
#40 Caring AND Agreem*
#41 Caregiver AND Agreem*

#42 Carer WITH planning
#43 Carers WITH planning
#44 Caring WITH planning
#45 Caregivers WITH planning
#46 Carer WITH Review
#47 Carers WITH Review
#48 Caring WITH Review
#49 Caregivers WITH Review
#50 Carer WITH Agreem*
#51 Carers WITH Agreem*
#52 Caring WITH Agreem*
#53 Caregiver WITH Agreem*
#54 Carer WITH assess*
#55 Carers WITH assess*
#56 Caring WITH assess*
#57 Caregiver WITH assess*
#58 Carer AND Involve*
#59 Carers AND Involve*
#60 Caring AND Involve*
#61 Caregiver AND Involve*
#62 Carer AND Inclus*
#63 Carers AND Inclus*
#64 Caring AND Inclus*
#65 Caregiver AND Inclus*

C2 SPECTR
#1 Carer
#2 Carer AND Particip*
#3 Carer OR particip*
#4 Carers AND particip*
#5 Carer AND inclus*
#6 Carers AND inclus*
#7 Carer OR inclus*
#8 Carers OR inclus*
#9 Carer OR involve*
#10 Carers OR involve*
#11 Carer AND involve*
#12 Carers AND involve*

Campbell Collaboration
#1 Carer
#2 Carer AND Particip*
#3 Carer OR particip*
#4 Carers AND particip*
#5 Carer AND inclus*
#6 Carers AND inclus*
#7 Carer OR inclus*
#8 Carers OR inclus*
#9 Carer OR involve*
#10 Carers OR involve*
#11 Carer AND involve*
#12 Carers AND involve*

ELSC (preset search menu)
#1 Carers
#2 Carers AND plann*
#3 Carers AND Partn*
#4 Carers AND assess*
#5 Carers WITH plann*
#6 Carers WITH partn*
#7 Carers OR plann*
#8 Carers OR partn*
#9 Carers OR assess*
#10 Caregiver

Zetoc -

#1 Carer
#2 Carer AND particip*
#3 Carers AND particip*
#4 Caring AND particip*
#5 Caregiver AND particip*
#6 Caregiver WITH particip*
#7 Carer WITH particip*
#8 Carers WITH Particip*
#9 Caring WITH particip*
#10 Carers AND involve*
#11 Carer AND Involve*
#12 Carers AND involve*
#13 Caregiver AND involve*
#14 Carer AND inclus*
#15 Carer AND inclus*
#16 Carers AND inclus*
#17 Caregiver AND inclus*
#18 Carer AND assess*
#19 Carer WITH assess*
#20 Caregiver AND assess*
#21 Caregiver WITH assess*
#22 Carers AND assess*
#23 Carers WITH assess*
#24 Carer AND plann*
#25 Carer WITH plann*
#26 Carers AND plann*
#27 Carers WITH plann*
#28 Caregivers AND plann*
#29 Caregivers WITH plann*
#30 Carer AND Plann*
#31 Carers AND Plann*
#32 Caring AND Plann*

#33 Caregiver AND Plann*
#34 Carer AND Partner*
#35 Carers AND Partner*
#36 Caring AND Partner*
#37 Caregiver AND Partner*
#38 Carer AND Agreem*
#39 Carers AND Agreem*
#40 Caring AND Agreem*
#41 Caregivers AND Agreem*
#42 Carer AND Review
#43 Carers AND Review
#44 Caring AND Review
#45 Caregiver AND Review
#46 Carer WITH Review
#47 Carers WITH Review
#48 Caring WITH Review
#49 Caregiver WITH Review
#50 Carer WITH Agreem*
#51 Carers WITH Agreem*
#52 Caring WITH Agreem*
#53 Caregiver WITH Agrem*
#54 Carer WITH Partner*
#55 Caring WITH Partner*
#56 Caregiver WITH Partner*
#57 Carer WITH Partner*
#58 Carers WITH Involv*
#59 Caring WITH Involv*
#60 Caregiver WITH Involv
#61 Carer WITH Involv*
#62 Carers WITH Inclus*
#63 Caring WITH Inclus*
#64 Caregiver WITH Inclus*
#65 Carer WITH Inclus*

IBSS

#1 Carer AND particip*
#2 Carers AND particip*
#3 Caring AND particip*
#4 Caregiver AND particip*
#5 Carer AND involve*
#6 Carers AND involve*
#7 Caring AND involve*
#8 Caregiver AND involve*
#9 Carer AND inclus*
#10 Carers AND inclus*
#11 Caring AND inclus*
#12 Caregiver AND inclus*
#13 Carer AND assess*
#14 Carers AND assess*
#15 Caring AND assess*
#16 Caregiver AND assess*
#17 Carer AND plann*
#18 Carers AND plann*
#19 Caring AND plann*
#20 Carer WITH particip*
#21 Carers WITH particip*
#22 Caring WITH particip*
#23 Caregiver WITH particip*

#24 Carer WITH Partner*
#25 Carers WITH Partner*
#26 Caring WITH Partner*
#27 Caregiver WITH Partner*
#28 Carer WITH Review
#29 Carers WITH Review
#30 Caring WITH Review
#31 Caregiving WITH Review
#32 Carer WITH Agreem*
#33 Carers WITH Agreem*
#34 Caring WITH Agreem
#35 Caregiver WITH Agreem

ISI Web of Knowledge

#1 Carer AND particip*
#2 Carers AND particip*
#3 Caring AND particip*
#4 Caregiver AND particip*
#5 Care AND involve*
#6 Carers AND involve*
#7 Caring AND involve*
#8 Caregiver AND involve*
#9 Carer AND inclus*
#10 Carers AND inclus*
#11 Caring AND inclus*
#12 Caregiver AND inclus*
#13 Carer AND assess*
#14 Carers AND assess*
#15 Caring AND assess*
#16 Caregiver AND assess*
#17 Carer AND plann*
#18 Carers AND plann*
#19 Caring AND plann*
#20 Caregiver AND plann*
#21 Carer WITH plann*
#22 Carers WITH plann*
#23 Caring WITH plann*
#24 Caregiver WITH plann*

#25 Carer WITH Partner*
#26 Carers WITH Partner*
#27 Caring WITH Partner*
#28 Caregiver WITH Partner*
#29 Carer WITH Review
#30 Carers WITH Review
#31 Caring WITH Review
#32 Caregiver WITH Review
#33 Carer WITH Agreem*
#34 Carers WITH Agreem*
#35 Caring WITH Agreem*
#36 Caregiver WITH Agreem*
#37 Carer AND Partner*
#38 Carers AND Partner*
#39 Caring AND Partner*
#40 Caregiver AND Partner*
#41 Carer AND Review
#42 Carers AND Review
#43 Caring AND Review
#44 Caregiver AND Review
#45 Carer AND Agreem*
#46 Carers AND Agreem*
#47 Caring AND Agreem*
#48 Caregiver AND Agreem*

OVID SIGLE

#1 Carer AND particip*
#2 Carers AND particip*
#3 Caring AND particip*
#4 Caregiver AND particip*
#5 Care AND involve*
#6 Carers AND involve*
#7 Caring AND involve*
#8 Caregiver AND involve*
#9 Carer AND inclus*
#10 Carers AND inclus*
#11 Caring AND inclus*
#12 Caregiver AND inclus*
#13 Carer AND assess*
#14 Carers AND assess*
#15 Caring AND assess*
#16 Caregiver AND assess*
#17 Carer AND plann*
#18 Carers AND plann*
#19 Caring AND plann*
#20 Caregiver AND plann*
#21 Carer WITH plann*
#22 Carers WITH plann*
#23 Caring WITH plann*
#24 Carer AND Review
#25 Carers AND Review
#26 Caring AND Review
#27 Caregiver AND Review
#28 Carer AND Partner*
#29 Carers AND Partner*
#30 Caring AND Partner*
#31 Caregiver AND Partner*
#32 Carer WITH Partner*
#33 Carers WITH Partner*
#34 Caring WITH Partner*
#35 Caregiver WITH Partner*
#36 Carer AND Agree*
#37 Carers AND Agree*
#38 Caring AND Agree*
#39 Caregiver AND Agree*

#40 Carer AND Partner*
#41 Carers AND Partner*
#42 Caring AND Partner*
#43 Caregiver AND Partner*
#44 Carer AND Review
#45 Carers AND Review
#46 Caring AND Review
#47 Caregiver AND Review
#48 Carer AND Agreem*
#49 Carers AND Agreem*
#50 Caring AND Agreem*
#51 Caregiver AND Agreem*
#52 Carer WITH Partner*
#53 Carers WITH Partner*
#54 Caring WITH Partner*
#55 Caregiver WITH Partner*
#56 Carer WITH Review
#57 Carers WITH Review
#58 Caring WITH Review
#59 Caregiver WITH Review
#60 Carer WITH Agreem*
#61 Carers WITH Agreem*
#62 Caring WITH Agreem*
#63 Caregiver WITH Agreem*
#64 Carer WITH plann*

PsycINFO

#1 Carer particip*
#2 Carer AND particip*
#3 Carers AND particip*
#4 Caring AND particip*
#5 Caregiver AND particip*
#6 Carer WITH particip*
#7 Carers WITH particip*
#8 Caring WITH particip*
#9 Caregiver WITH particip*
#10 Carer AND involve*
#11 Carers AND involve*
#12 Caring AND involve*
#13 Caregiver AND involve*
#14 Carer WITH involve*
#15 Carers WITH involve*
#16 Caring WITH involve*
#17 Caregiver WITH involve*
#18 Carer WITH inclus*
#19 Carers WITH inclus*
#20 Caring WITH inclus*
#21 Caregiver WITH inclus*
#22 Carer AND assess*
#23 Carers AND assess*
#24 Caring AND assess*
#25 Caregiver AND assess*
#26 Carer WITH assess*
#27 Carers WITH assess*
#28 Caring WITH assess*
#29 Caregiver WITH assess*
#30 Carer AND plann*
#31 Carers AND plann*
#32 Caring AND plann*

#33 Caregiver AND plann*
#34 Carer WITH plann*
#35 Carers WITH plann*
#36 Caring WITH plann*
#37 Caregiver WITH plann*
#38 Carer AND Partner*
#39 Carers AND Partner*
#40 Caring AND Partner*
#41 Caregiver AND Partner*
#42 Carer AND Review
#43 Carers AND Review
#44 Caring AND Review
#45 Caregiver AND Review
#46 Carer AND Agreem*
#47 Carers AND Agreem*
#48 Caring AND Agreem*
#49 Caregiver AND Agreem*
#50 Carer WITH Agreem*
#51 Carers WITH Agreem*
#52 Caring WITH Agreem*
#53 Caregiver WITH Agreem*
#54 Carer WITH Review
#55 Carers WITH Review
#56 Caring WITH Review
#57 Caregiver WITH REview
#58 Carer WITH Partner*
#59 Carers WITH Partner*
#60 Caring WITH Partner*
#61 Caregiver WITH Partner*

CSA Illumina (ASSIA, ERIC, Social Services Abstracts, Sociological Abstracts)

#1 Carer

#2 Carer Particip*

#3 Carer AND Particip*

#4 Carers AND Particip*

#5 Caring AND Particip*

#6 Caregiver AND Particip*

#7 Carer AND Inclus*

#8 Carers AND Inclus*

#9 Caregiver AND Inclus*

#10 Carer AND Involve*

#11 Carers AND Involve*

#12 Caring AND Involve*

#13 Caregiver AND Involve*

#14 Carer AND Assess*

#15 Carers AND Assess*

#16 Caring AND Assess*

#17 Caregiver AND Assess*

#18 Carer AND Plann*

#19 Carers AND Plann*

#20 Caring AND Plann*

#21 Caregiver AND Plann*

#22 Carer AND Review

#23 Carers AND Review

#24 Caring AND Review

#25 Caregiver AND Review

#26 Carer AND Partner*

#27 Caregiver AND Partner*

#28 CarersAND Partner*

#29 Caring AND Partner*

#30 Carer AND Agreem*

#31 Carers AND Agreem*

#32 Caring AND Agreem*

#33 Caregiver AND Agreem

4 carer permutations WITH particip*, Inclus* Involve, Assess* Plann*, Review, Partner*, and Agreem*

Cinahl (Ovid Gateway)

#1 Carer particip*
#2 Carer AND particip*
#3 Carers AND particip*
#4 Caring AND particip*
#5 Caregiver AND particip*
#6 Carer WITH particip*
#7 Carers WITH particip*
#8 Caring WITH particip*
#9 Caregiver WITH particip*
#10 Carer AND involve*
#11 Carers AND involve*
#12 Caring AND involve*
#13 Caregiver AND involve*
#14 Carer WITH involve*
#15 Carers WITH involve*
#16 Caring WITH involve*
#17 Caregiver WITH involve*
#18 Carer WITH inclus*
#19 Carers WITH inclus*
#20 Caring WITH inclus*
#21 Caregiver WITH inclus*
#22 Carer AND assess*
#23 Carers AND assess*
#24 Caring AND assess*
#25 Caregiver AND assess*
#26 Carer WITH assess*
#27 Carers WITH assess*
#28 Caring WITH assess*
#29 Caregiver WITH assess*
#30 Carer AND plann*
#31 Carers AND plann*
#32 Caring AND plann*

#33 Caregiver AND plann*
#34 Carer WITH plann*
#35 Carers WITH plann*
#36 Caring WITH plann*
#37 Caregiver WITH plann*
#38 Carer AND Partner*
#39 Carers AND Partner*
#40 Caring AND Partner*
#41 Caregiver AND Partner*
#42 Carer AND Review
#43 Carers AND Review
#44 Caring AND Review
#45 Caregiver AND Review
#46 Carer AND Agreem*
#47 Carers AND Agreem*
#48 Caring AND Agreem*
#49 Caregiver AND Agreem*
#50 Carer WITH Agreem*
#51 Carers WITH Agreem*
#52 Caring WITH Agreem*
#53 Caregiver WITH Agreem*
#54 Carer WITH Review
#55 Carers WITH Review
#56 Caring WITH Review
#57 Caregiver WITH REview
#58 Carer WITH Partner*
#59 Carers WITH Partner*
#60 Caring WITH Partner*
#61 Caregiver WITH Partner*

Appendix D: Literature review: hand searches

Hand searches were carried out with the following journals:

Ageing & Society
Critical Social Policy: A Journal of Theory and Practice in Social Welfare
Disability & Society
European Journal of Social Work
Health & Social Care in the Community
International Social Work
Journal of Advanced Nursing
Journal of Interprofessional Care
Journal of Mental Health
Journal of Public Health Medicine
Journal of Social Policy
*Journal of Social Work Practice: Psychotherapeutic Approaches in Health, Welfare
    and the Community*
Mental Health Care
Practice: Journal of the BASW
Professional Nurse: From Policy to Practice
Race and Ethnicity
Research, Policy and Planning
Social Policy and Society
Social Policy & Administration: An International Journal of Policy and Research
Social Work Education
Social Work in Europe
The British Journal of Social Work
The Journal of Dementia Care

Appendix E: National organisations

The Afiya Trust (www.afiya-trust.org.uk)
Alzheimer's Society (www.alzheimers.org.uk)
Alzheimer's Society Lesbian and Gay Carers Network (www.alzheimers.org.uk/Gay_
    Carers/_
The British Council of Disabled People (BCODP) (www.bcdop.org.uk)
Carers Network
Carers UK (formerly Carers National Association) (www.carersuk.org/)
Chest, Heart, Stroke Association (CHSA)
Crossroads – Caring for Carers (www.crossroads.org.uk/)
Depression Alliance (www.depressionalliance.org/)
Disability Action (www.disabilityaction.org)
King's Fund (www.kingsfund.org.uk)
Manic Depression Fellowship (MDF): The BiPolar organisation (www.mdf.org.uk)
MENCAP (www.mencap.org.uk)
MIND (www.mind.org.uk)
Multiple Sclerosis Society (MS) (www.mssociety.org.uk/)
People First (www.peoplefirst.org.uk)
Princess Royal Trust for Carers (www.carers.org/)
Rethink (formerly National Schizophrenia Fellowship) (www.rethink.org/)
Social Care Institute for Excellence (SCIE) (www.scie.org.uk/)
The Terrence Higgins Trust (www.tht.org.uk/)

Appendix F: Article summary sheet

Number_____ Author _____

Title _____

Journal_____

Location _____ Context _____

Type of carer _____

Type of user _____

Ethnic group_____

Type of data   Conceptual   Empirical   Descriptive

_____

_____

Aim of study _____

_____

Research type _____

Sample _____

Methods _____

Participation_____

_____

Key findings _____

_____

Implications for _____

service delivery _____

_____

Relevance _____

Comments _____

Appendix G: Methods adopted in the SCIE Position Paper on carer participation

General overview comments

The Position Paper brought together a systematic literature and wide-reaching practice survey on carer participation. The terms 'participation', 'involvement' and 'inclusion' were all used to capture the range of understandings and terminology likely to be used. The details of the literature review are spelled out in Section 1.1.1 of this Position Paper. Details of the practice survey follow.

The design, operationalisation and review elements of the Position Paper and the overall progress of the research were guided by two key review bodies:

* **Carer participation review group (CPRG)** This provided day-to-day and largely street-level insights into the reality of the carer experience and helped firm up the research focus and design in a way that would be better understood by carers. The group consisted of 10 members: four research team members and six carers from North East England who were affiliated to the Sunderland Carers' Centre and their national network, the Princess Royal Trust. This group, which met five times during the lifetime of the research, has proven invaluable in aiding the progress of the research.
* **Research review group** In addition to the day-to-day reality check provided by the CPRG above, the research team also established a 'national' (England, Wales and Northern Ireland) research review group to provide more strategic policy, practice and programme insights. Their experience embraced DH-grounded work on carers of people with learning difficulties, BME-inclusive carer working, insights into carers in Northern Ireland and Wales, gay and lesbian carer issues and lifetime carer issues. Meeting three times during the lifetime of the project, the research review group provided the strategic steer towards SCIE and wider social care benchmarks, while providing detailed guidance on how to maximise the coverage and depth of the research for both the literature review and practice survey. This group, like the CPRG, has been central to the decision-making processes of the research.

The researchers also sought guidance on issues that were outwith the research review group's expertise – for example, informal carers who are also in paid employment.

Rationale and nature of the practice survey

Taking direction from the SCIE review specification and carers' views, the practice survey aimed to identify, capture and report best practice in carer participation and the factors that continue to mitigate against the adoption of best practice. In addition to best practice, the survey design aimed to maximise the geographical spread of responses and practice under review so as to avoid skewing the findings towards a particular region or area. However, this may simply have provided practice data that was a shadow variable of the good practice more generally in a given area/ region. As with the literature review, the practice survey spread was facilitated by a corroborated grading of a given statutory organisation using a three-star system. These star ratings are not meant to represent official measures as per SSI inspections ratings, but are useful operational indicators employed to select for further study. They are based loosely on a amalgam of ideas from Goss and Miller (81) and the Audit Commission (154) continuum mentioned earlier:

- **No stars** Authority is doing **little** in the way of carer participation. Little or no evidence of partnership working; basic consultation only.
- **One star** Authority is doing some **limited** or **early** carer participation work. Some evidence of actual or planned partnership working.
- **Two stars** Authority is doing a **significant** amount of carer participation. Established partnerships usually in place; sound feedback and change agency monitoring in place.
- **Three stars** Authority is doing **substantial** and **exemplary** best practice work on carer participation. Mature and successful partnership working; innovative feedback and change agency monitoring.

The practice survey design
Following the research design outlined in the SCIE bid and carer commentary from the CPRG and research review group, the practice survey took the form of a two-stage process.

Stage 1 was a **scoping survey questionnaire** sent to identified statutory and voluntary sector organisations (including carers' centres). It aimed to 'identify, detail and delineate the range and depth of carer participation practices' (bid document excerpt). In the initial tranche, 629 questionnaires were despatched by email with a covering letter that explained the research and its context. A special email return address was established to ensure the capture of incoming mail. A follow-up email questionnaire was despatched to any non-respondents to the first tranche. A total of 1,109 questionnaires were despatched in the two tranches.

The following sources were used to identify suitable respondents:

- *The Social Services Yearbook 2003/04*
- *The Health Services Yearbook 2003/04*
- *The Voluntary Sector Handbook 2004*
- Princess Trust affiliated organisations database

Stage 2 comprised **telephone interviews** with a range of respondent organisations. The research team completed 47 interviews with people from SSDs, PCTs, health authorities, PBs and carers' centres.

The interviews with carers themselves (*n*=18) were carried out by other carers who belonged to or were close to the CPRG. As this group of carer interviewees were the only ones directly engaged in caring, it was felt that interview matching and sensitivity would be enhanced by using other carers to interview them. Indeed members of the CPRG were instrumental in involving carers in these interview contexts. The carer interviewers were trained in interview techniques by the research team, and agreed research protocols were adhered to. An iterative interview checking process was put in place to ensure that inter-interview comparability and standards were maintained.

Stage 1

The CPRG, with support from the research team, drew up a number of questions that they felt were benchmarks for evincing best practice in carer participation. Questionnaires incorporating these benchmarks were then emailed to the following as per the Position Paper specification:

- all SSDs/health boards in England, Wales and Northern Ireland
- a selection of PCTs, acute health trusts and mental health trusts
- a selection of LDPBs.

With reference to trusts and PBs, there are many hundreds of these and the decision was taken to contact a selection based on geographical spread, with at least one authority in all the regions listed in Appendix I. Selection in the health arena also aimed to include a range of primary health, teaching, mental health, acute and mixed (adult and children's) trusts. PBs were selected midway through the completion of this Position Paper and were targeted by region and, where possible, to match a responding SSD and carers' centre.

Response rates

Statutory organisation	Number (Qs) despatched	Number returned (valid)	Percentage (valid)
SSD	164 (all)	67	41%
PCT/health authority	108 (selection)	32 (16/16)	30%
Health and social care trust and board, JCT	17	10	60%
LDPB	37	9	25%

In addition to the above statutory organisations, the practice survey also sought the views of a selection of carers' organisations and carers themselves. These views would help corroborate, test or qualify statutory commentaries. In all, 105 carers' centres were contacted, with a valid response coming from 16 (15%). This was a disappointing response rate compared to that of the statutory sector, but may be explicable in terms of the 'best practice' focus of the research, which required cross-comparisons that may have been difficult for individual carer's centres. That it is the role of the statutory sector (SSDs and PCTs) as lead funders to provide official evaluations of the extent and effectiveness of carer participation may have also been a pervasive view. This may explain the poor response rate (5%) from the voluntary sector, many of whom are campaign organisations and do not provide frontline services.

The first three types of organisations in the response rate table above – SSDs, PCTs and health authorities – received the same questionnaire requesting that they reflect critically on their activity in carer participation. LDPBs, in addition to those sorts of questions, were also asked to focus on lifetime caring situations. In addition to evaluating the effectiveness of carer participation and partnership working in their locality, carers' centres were asked to comment on their own good practice as well as that of the social services and health partners with whom they worked. The questionnaires mainly requested yes/no answers, but allowed respondents to detail their practice and their interface with statutory services. Respondents were also asked if they would be willing to take part in telephone interviews.

Selecting Stage 2 respondents

Stage 2 questionnaire respondents were selected purposively by the CPRG, with the guidance of the core research team, to provide:

* a range, depth and variety of practice activity and effectiveness (SSDs, PCTs, health authorities and PBs)
* a range of frontline carer support activity and key corroborative evidence to test the above statutory claims (carers' centres, carers, major voluntary sector organisations).

As the largest respondents' group, SSDs were graded using the three-star system detailed above. Twenty SSD organisation interviews were identified, involving all those graded with three stars plus a selection of two-, one- and non-starred questionnaires.

PCTs and health boards (a total of 10 interviews), PBs (5 interviews), and carers' centres (10 interviews) were selected on the basis of a defined geographical spread to maximise coverage within England, Wales and Northern Ireland. Where possible, these interviews were matched to known SSD interviews by locality.

It was initially envisaged that carers' interview contacts would be routed via eligible Stage 2 SSDs. However, delay in receiving clearance from the ADSS to complete this element led to an alternative method of contact via carers' centres directly (15 interviews). Geographical mapping with SSDs, PCTs and PBs was undertaken wherever possible.

Stage 2

Once selected, interviews took place between October 2004 and January 2005. The completion date was later than had first been envisaged but was shaped by the time required to obtain ADSS clearance for SSD and PB interviews. All 63 interviews were completed successfully and provided a rich evidence base with which to begin to triangulate (link) data from Stage 2 (interviews) and Stage 1 (scoping survey questionnaire).

These triangulated findings are laid out in the executive summary of the Position Paper. Interview coverage was largely good in England and Wales but somewhat less successful in Northern Ireland,with statutory interviews only. However, evidence gained via a member of the research review group from Northern Ireland helped link supporting data to the questionnaire responses from health and social care boards in Northern Ireland.

Appendix H: Carers' organisation responses and their statutory partners

Total: 16 carers' centres

Question

In your locality, do your statutory partners involve carers in any or all stages of service planning or delivery?

Organisation	Yes	No	Don't know	Total
SSD	13	1	2	16 (16)
PCT	4	2	10	16 (16)
NHS trust	0	1	15	16 (16)

Question

Do carers have direct access to key decision-making forums in your partner agencies?

Organisation	Yes	No	Don't know	Total
SSD	10	2	4	16 (16)
PCT	6	3	7	16 (16)
NHS trust	6	2	7	15 (+ 1 nil response)

Question

Do your partner agencies set out in key documents how you are going to include/involve carers?

Organisation	Yes	No	Don't know	Total
SSD	9	0	7	16
PCT	6	3	7	16
NHS trust	0	1	14	16

Question

Do your partner agencies ensure that carers can influence service planning and delivery in a way that is accountable to others?

Organisation	Yes	No	Don't know	Total
SSD	10	0	6	16
PCT	5	2	9	16
NHS trust	4	2	10	16

Question

Do your partner agencies make resources available for carers to be actively involved/included?

Organisation	Yes	No	Don't know	Totals
SSD	9	1	6	16 (16)
PCT	4	1	11	16 (16)
NHS trust	0	1	15	16 (16)

Question

Do your partner agencies have a written policy for including carers who are likely to be marginalised – e.g. people who do not recognise themselves as carers, black/minority ethnic carers, gay and lesbian carers?

Organisation	Yes	No	Don't know	Total
SSD	6	1	9	16 (16)
PCT	4	1	11	16 (16)
NHS trust	2	1	13	16 (16)

Question

Do your partner agencies agree with carers what outcomes (changes) youare looking for in the planning and delivery of services?

Organisation	Yes	No	Don't know	Total
SSD	3	3	10	16 (16)
PCT	2	3	11	16 (16)
NHS trust	2	3	11	16 (16)

Question

Do your partner agencies agree a period of time with carers when you will review these outcomes to see whether they have been achieved?

Organisation	Yes	No	Don't know	Total
SSD	2	4	10	16 (16)
PCT	2	4	10	16 (16)
NHS trust	1	4	11	16 (16)

Question

If your partner agencies carry out carers' assessments, have they sought feedback on the process of those assessments?

Organisation	Yes	No	Don't know	Total
SSD	4	3	9	16 (16)
PCT	1	4	11	16 (16)
NHS trust	0	2	14	16 (16)

Question

If your partner agencies carry out carers' assessments, have they sought feedback on the content of those assessments?

Organisation	Yes	No	Don't know	Total
SSD	2	3	11	16 (16)
PCT	1	2	13	16 (16)
NHS trust	1	2	13	16 (16)

Question

Do the employees of your partner agencies receive training in carer involvement/ inclusion?

Organisation	Yes	No	Don't know	Total
SSD	6	1	9	16 (16)
PCT	5	1	10	16 (16)
NHS trust	1	2	13	16 (16)

Appendix I: Geographical response rates from statutory organisations, excluding learning disability partnership boards

The following is a brief overview of the geographical spread of responses. The data are presented by 'region' or area, as opposed to city/town, as they aim to protect the identity of given respondent organisations yet illustrate the range and coverage of responses and, in a small number of instances, the limits to the research coverage. Counties are provided where they help illustrate the boundaries being applied – for example, in and around London.

Regions and areas were identified as follows, with corresponding numbers of statutory responses:

17 **London boroughs**
11 **South East England**: Kent, Surrey, Sussex, Buckinghamshire, Oxfordshire, Hertfordshire, Essex
4 **Southern England**: Hampshire, Dorset
13 **English Midlands**: Staffordshire, South/Mid Derbyshire, Nottinghamshire, Warwickshire, Leicestershire, West Midlands
10 **Eastern England**: Cambridgeshire, Lincolnshire, Suffolk, Humberside
5 **Pennines**: Yorkshire and North Derbyshire
14 **North West**: Lancashire, Cheshire, Cumbria, North West conurbation
16 **North East**: Tyne, Wear, Teesside, Northumberland
9 **South West England**: Avon and Somerset, Cornwall, Devon, Wiltshire, Gloucestershire
1 **North Wales**
4 **South Wales**
1 **Mid-Wales**
4 **Northern Ireland**

Appendix J: Examples of documentation that include references to a commitment to involving and including carers

- Carers' strategy
- NSF implementation documents
- Local strategic partnerships
- All key strategy and policy documents
- Commissioning strategy
- Consultation strategy
- Learning disability strategy
- Mental health carers' strategy
- Departmental strategic plan
- Multiagency commitment plan
- Carers' quality standards group
- Joint investment plan learning disabilities plan
- Service plans
- Carers' support team plan
- User/carer involvement policy
- Adult social care action plan
- Multiagency carers' strategy
- User and carer consultation and engagement framework

Appendix K: Examples of key decision-making forums that give carers direct access to service planning and delivery decisions

- Through being chair of the carers' forum
- Carers' sub-group of LIT
- Through membership of carers' forum
- Carer members of cancer and palliative care review board
- Through board meetings – for example, joint health and social care
- Advocacy partnership group
- Carers' modernisation team
- Parent carers' forum
- Mental health carers' forum
- Three times yearly meetings with director of SSD, when issues not resolved at lower level can be put to director
- Carers' strategy group
- Multiagency carers strategy group
- Carers' sub-group of PB
- Health and social care improvement board
- Regular bi-monthly forums open to carers of
    > older people
    > people with mental health problems
    > people with learning and/or physical disability
    > Young children with disabilities.

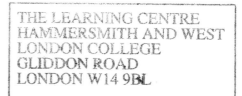

Other guides available from SCIE

HAS SERVICE USER PARTICIPATION MADE A DIFFERENCE TO SOCIAL CARE SERVICES?
Sarah Carr
ISBN 1 904812 10 4
March 2004
Ordering code: PP03

INVOLVING SERVICE USERS AND CARERS IN SOCIAL WORK EDUCATION
Enid Levin
ISBN 1 904812 07 4
March 2004
Ordering code: RG02

IMPLEMENTING THE CARERS (EQUAL OPPORTUNITIES) ACT 2004
Elaine Cass
October 2005
Ordering code: PG05

To order any of these publications please contact:

Communications Team
Social Care Institute for Excellence
Goldings House
2 Hay's Lane
London SE1 2HB

tel: 020 7089 6840